Contexts in Literature

The Literature of Love

Mary Ward

Series editor: Adrian Barlow

CAMBRIDGE
UNIVERSITY PRESS

CAMBRIDGE UNIVERSITY PRESS
Cambridge, New York, Melbourne, Madrid, Cape Town, Singapore, São Paulo, Delhi

Cambridge University Press
The Edinburgh Building, Cambridge CB2 8RU, UK

www.cambridge.org
Information on this title: www.cambridge.org/9780521729819

First published 2009

Printed in the United Kingdom at the University Press, Cambridge

A catalogue record for this publication is available from the British Library

ISBN 978-0-521-72981-9 paperback

Editorial management: Gill Stacey

Cover illustration: 'Le Champ de Mars' by Chagall, Marc 1953–54 (detail)
© ADAGP, Paris and DACS, London 2007.

Contents

Introduction

Why is it that the most unoriginal thing we can say to each other is still the thing we long to hear? 'I love you' is always a quotation.

(Jeanette Winterson *Written on the Body*, 1994)

He loved me, I loved him, his presence effaced all other presences; we were happy, then he stopped loving me and I suffered.

(Collette *Bella Vista*, 1937)

Finally he spoke the three simple words that no amount of bad faith or bad art can ever quite cheapen. She repeated them, with exactly the same slight emphasis on the second word, as though she were the one to say them first. He had no religious belief but it was impossible not to think of an unseen presence or witness in the room, and that these words spoken aloud were like signatures on an unseen contract.

(Ian McEwan *Atonement*, 2001)

The scope of this book is defined by these three extracts. *The Literature of Love* examines the expression of love in literature: the ways in which 'I love you' is said and how words are shaped to convey this expression. It also traces the narrative of desire in literature from the first intimations of love through to the endings, whether happy or sad. We, as readers, are McEwan's 'unseen presence or witness' as we engage with the text. As the schoolteacher Hector observes in the play, *The History Boys* (2004), by Alan Bennett:

The best moments in reading are when you come across something – a thought, a feeling, a way of looking at things – which you had thought special and particular to you. Now here it is, set down by someone else, a person you have never met, someone even who is long dead. And it is as if a hand has come out and taken yours.

This book explores ways of reading the literature of love, first by providing a brief survey of the philosophical, cultural and theological contexts of Western love literature. However, 'I love you' centres this book. Through connections and comparisons, it attempts to consider questions such as: What do writers mean by love? How is passion expressed in literary texts? How do lovers (and poets) invent new worlds? Is love ever demonic? What about the end of love?

How this book is organised

Part 1: Approaching the literature of love

Significant contextual influences from European literature are introduced to illustrate the starting points: the philosophical and religious ideas, the archetypes and symbols which later writers have used as the basis for their own explorations of love. The writers discussed include Plato, Ovid, Chaucer and Petrarch.

Part 2: Approaching the texts

Different texts are considered and compared thematically. The topics range from passion and desire, through courtship, marriage, honeymoon and married love to betrayal and loss. Different forms of writing about love – for example, the *epithalamion*, the elegy – and different expressions from the tragic to the comic are introduced and discussed.

Part 3: Texts and extracts

Part 3 contains extracts from poetry, prose and drama discussed elsewhere in the book. The passages illustrate the varieties of love and the different ways of experiencing and writing about love encountered in Parts 1 and 2, and provide material for later discussion in Parts 4 and 5.

Part 4: Critical approaches

Part 4 outlines a range of critical and theoretical approaches which may be employed when analysing passages of writing about the literature of love. Different approaches to texts such as *Brideshead Revisited* and writers such as D.H. Lawrence are discussed.

Part 5: How to write about the literature of love

Part 5 offers guidance on writing about the literature of love. It focuses on comparisons of thematically linked extracts of similar and contrasting genres.

Part 6: Resources

This part contains guidance on further reading and research, a glossary and index. (Terms which appear in the glossary are highlighted in bold type when they first appear in the main text.)

At different points throughout the book, and at the end of Parts 1 and 5, there are tasks and assignments designed to help the reader reflect on ideas discussed in the text.

1 | Approaching the literature of love

- What are the earliest sources for the literature of love?

- How did Plato define the nature of love?

- How has the Bible influenced the ways writers write about love?

- Who are the key medieval and Renaissance figures in the literature of love?

Authors – poets, dramatists, philosophers, novelists and letter writers – have always looked to their predecessors to help them understand and explain the emotions and the experiences of love. So too have readers. The literature of the past continues to influence the literature of the present as strongly as ever, and this literature is not insular: the metaphors, images and archetypes that constantly recur in English literary writing are drawn from all over Europe and beyond. Approaching the literature of love therefore needs to start by revisiting some of the key writers and key texts of European literature.

Plato

Plato, the Greek philosopher who lived *c.* 429–347 BC, founded the Academy, a school of philosophical enquiry, in Athens. Socrates was his teacher, and Plato in turn taught Aristotle. Great truths about what love is are thrashed out in a series of Dialogues in which Socrates takes the lead as teacher and mentor. In order to shape the listener's understanding, the imagery is helpfully physical, visceral and humorous. Two of the most famous Dialogues are the *Symposium*, a post-dinner party conversation, and *Phaedrus,* a country ramble.

Platonic love: the *Symposium* and *Phaedrus*

Our 21st-century understanding of a 'platonic' relationship is, usually, of a heterosexual friendship, high-minded and non-physical. It was the Renaissance philosopher Marsilio Ficino who introduced the term *Amor Platonicus* to define Platonic love as love of the divine. However, extracts from the *Symposium* and *Phaedrus* reveal that Platonic love in 5th-century Athens BC meant love between men, often an older and much younger man, that sexual intercourse might have been included, and that true love is a desire for the transcendent good. Four extended metaphors or analogies help readers to understand the nature of this love.

The first analogy occurs in the *Symposium*. Aristophanes, 'a writer of comedies', delights the guests with his own creation myth, a metaphorical 'spin' (literally) on our universal quest for the perfect partner:

> In the beginning, there were three sexes, male, female and hermaphrodite: male, the offspring of the sun, female of the earth, and the hermaphrodite, or half and half, the moon. They were circular to match their parents. 'Each human being formed a complete whole, with four hands, four legs and two faces'. When they ran they 'rolled along at high speed, like people doing cartwheels'. Zeus punished their audacity in attempting to attack the gods, by chopping these rotund beings in half 'like someone slicing vegetables for pickling'. Once they were split in half, they clung desperately to their 'other half' until they withered and died from weariness and hunger. Zeus had compassion on these wretched creatures, and made sure that their genitals were functioning properly so that they could get together. This is why we feel love for others: we are literally searching for our 'other half'.
>
> (translated by Tom Griffith, 1988)

The comedy in this charming myth emphasises its purpose: the pursuit of physical completeness. Aristophanes concludes by calling this *eros* or desire. This love is mortal and finite. It both objectifies the beloved and desires to possess.

Plato enlarges our understanding of the nature of *eros* through Socrates, who reports the wise teachings of Diotima. She questions whether lovers are simply people in search of their other half, and instead introduces a moral dimension: 'Love is the desire for the permanent possession of the good.' We may crave immortality, physically though the production of children, or mentally and spiritually through our thoughts and intellectual achievements. These may be great poems or our deeds of justice, as good citizens. The image of a ladder, the second analogy, is introduced in the *Symposium* by Diotima in a mystical speech on the Ascent of Love. She envisages

> ... climbing from the love of one person to the love of two; from two to love of all physical beauty; from physical beauty to beauty in human behaviour; thence to beauty in subjects of study; from them he arrives finally at that branch of knowledge which studies nothing but ultimate beauty. Then at last he understands what true beauty is ... He will see divine beauty in its unique essence ... It exists for all time, by itself and with itself, unique. All other forms of beauty derive from it.

The third metaphor, a vivid pictorial image of desire, occurs in *Phaedrus*. The young man, Phaedrus, is in dialogue with Socrates. He is profoundly impressed by a magnificent speech he has just heard which claims that, paradoxically, you should have a physical relationship with someone who doesn't love you, because all lovers are absurd and irrational – mad! However, Socrates proves that love is actually a good thing. It may be madness but it is a good type of madness.

Therefore, by means of an extended analogy, Plato provides a model for the operation of love:

> The soul is made up of three elements; the tripartite soul. The chariot is the body, and the charioteer is the reasoning part of the soul. The charioteer controls two horses, one good and one bad. The good horse is described as 'well proportioned, with a high neck. It is restrained and modest, has never felt the whip and is easy to control.' On the other hand the bad horse is a 'jumble of parts'. It is 'slow to obey even whip and spur together and is the companion of excess and boasting'. The good horse represents the noble, emotional, high-minded side of the soul or desire, whereas the bad horse is basic physical appetite: 'When the charioteer first sees the face he loves, warming his whole soul with the sight, he begins to be filled with tickling and pains of desire.' The two horses react in utterly contradictory ways. 'The good horse is modest, controlled and restrained whereas the bad horse charges violently forward to possess the beloved and has to be vigorously restrained.'
>
> The charioteer sees the radiant image of the divine reflected in the beauty of the young man. Numinous imagery is used; he is *dazzled*: the sight fills him with *fear*; 'he falls back, overcome with *awe*'. A ferociously bloody power struggle then ensues between the 'bad' horse and the charioteer. Eventually, the bad horse is humbled and the way is paved for the lover to 'worship' the boy.

Finally, a fourth analogy develops this idea.

> When a man sees beauty here, in this life, he is reminded of true beauty. He grows wings, and stands there fluttering them, eager to fly upwards, but unable to do so. Yet still he looks upwards, as birds do, and takes no notice of what is below; and so he is accused of being mad.

Why is he rooted to the spot? Socrates' conclusion is comforting: 'Of all forms of divine possession, this is the best – and has the best origins – both for him who has it and for him who shares in it. It is this madness which the lover of beauty must experience if he is to be called a lover.' He is dimly aware of the perfect beauty he has seen in heaven, unencumbered with a body, in the **World of Forms**. He begins to grow wings of desire. Plato equates the physical discomfort of growing wings with that of cutting teeth. The transcendent is rooted in the body.

Plato's influence

Plato continues to be hugely influential in Western literature. As we have seen, the *Symposium* and *Phaedrus* explore, through dialogue, the relationship between beauty, desire and love. Earthly beauty is a pale shadow of absolute perfect beauty. Therefore the Platonic lover worships the beauty of his mistress so that he may adore her soul. Plato's influence is to be seen in the courtly love tradition, Petrarchan love poetry, Renaissance and metaphysical poetry, particularly Shakespeare's sonnets and the poetry of John Donne. Indeed, much of Donne's poetry is influenced by Platonic thought. In 'The Good Morrow', the poet celebrates the true maturity of his love in Platonic terms, echoing the World of Forms:

> If ever any beauty I did see,
> Which I desired and got, 'twas but a dream of thee.

The first movement of composer John Adam's *Harmonium* (1980) is a setting of another Donne poem. Adams states: 'I settled on three poems of transcendental vision. "Negative Love" examines the qualities of various forms of love, ascending in the manner of Plato's *Symposium,* from the carnal to the divine.'

▶ Compare 'Negative Love' with 'No Platonique Love' by William Cartwright (Part 3, pages 77 and 78). Which do you consider comes closer to Platonic thinking?

The Bible

The Bible has been one of the most important sources for writers and artists depicting different facets of love: platonic, spiritual and sexual. Every aspect of love is to be found in its pages: Adam and Eve as 'one flesh', the fraternal love of David and Jonathan and the poetic eroticism of the *Song of Songs*. In the New Testament the Virgin Mary, Jesus' mother, weeps at the foot of the Cross and Christ's own sacrifice demonstrates God's love for humankind. This sacrificial love, a love which gives freely of itself, and which yearns for the good of the other is called *agape*; it is distinct from *eros,* the love which desires both possession of, and union with, the beloved.

Bible narratives have provided Western literature with a language of love. They have influenced writers as diverse as Milton in the 17th century after the English Civil War, and American playwright Tony Kushner (*Angels in America*, see Part 2, page 43) writing at the height of the AIDS epidemic in the early 1990s.

The Old Testament

Adam and Eve

Adam means 'earth' in Hebrew, as, according to Genesis Chapters 2 and 3, he was created from 'the dust of the ground'; Eve means 'life' as she is the mother of all living things. She was formed from one of Adam's ribs.

> And Adam said, This is now bone of my bones, and flesh of my
> flesh: she shall be called Woman, because she was taken out of Man.
> Therefore shall a man leave his father and mother, and shall cleave
> unto his wife: and they shall be one flesh. And they were both naked,
> the man and his wife and were not ashamed.
>
> (Genesis 2, 23–25)

Adam and Eve cultivate Eden, the garden of earthly delights. After being tempted by the serpent into disobeying God by eating 'of the fruit of the tree of the knowledge of good and evil', they plunge into fruitless mutual recrimination: 'The woman whom thou gavest to be with me, she gave me of the tree, and I did eat,' Adam complains. They lose their immortality and an angel with a fiery sword drives them from Eden, their paradise on earth. Eve and her female descendants have to suffer the pangs of childbirth; Adam must work 'in the sweat of his face', until he returns 'unto the ground'.

In this story, Adam at first displays a proudly possessive intimacy through the repetition of 'bone' and 'flesh'. However, he later coldly dissociates himself from Eve, calling her 'the woman whom thou gavest to be with me'. In Book 9 of his **epic** poem *Paradise Lost* (published 1667) John Milton describes the romantic love of Adam and Eve, which is put to the test after Satan, in the guise of a serpent, has deceived Eve. Adam, as yet unfallen, meets flushed and intoxicated Eve after she has eaten the forbidden fruit.

▶ How does Adam express his love for Eve during this encounter? What connects Milton's writing with the depiction of Adam and Eve in Genesis? (See Part 3, page 78.)

'One flesh'

The Marriage Service, in *The Book of Common Prayer*, contains this phrase from Genesis: 'these two, man and wife, shall become one flesh'. Writers from Donne onwards have explored this mystery:

> But as all several souls contain
> Mixture of things, they know not what,
> Love, these mixed souls doth mix again,
> And makes both one, each this and that.
>
> (from John Donne 'The Extasie')

'My love for Heathcliff resembles the eternal rocks beneath ... I am Heathcliff – he's always, always in my mind – not as a pleasure, any more than I am always a pleasure to myself – but as my own being.'

(from *Wuthering Heights*)

'The Extasie' defines the union as a mystical–alchemical process, with Love as the alchemist (reflected in the logical precision of the lines), whereas Cathy speaks about her love for Heathcliff as something sublime, elemental and eternal. W.H. Auden, in the poem 'Lullaby' (1937), hints that lovers may, fleetingly, experience union of body and soul:

Soul and body have no bounds:
To lovers as they lie upon
Her tolerant enchanted slope
In their ordinary swoon,
Grave the vision Venus sends
Of supernatural sympathy
Universal love and hope.

David and Jonathan

Another major story from the Old Testament, to which writers on love have returned again and again, is the story of David and Jonathan. David, on learning that Jonathan and his father King Saul have been killed fighting the Philistines, enemies of the Israelites, utters this elegy:

The beauty of Israel is slain upon the high places: how are the mighty fallen ... Saul and Jonathan were lovely and pleasant in their lives, and in their death they were not divided: they were swifter than eagles, they were stronger than lions ...

I am distressed for thee, my brother Jonathan: very pleasant hast thou been unto me: thy love to me was wonderful, passing the love of women. (II Samuel 1, vv.19, 23, 26)

Dying on the battlefield gives Saul and Jonathan undying honour. David elevates them into personified 'Beauty': eagles and lions have an archetypal nobility. The last sentence reads as a personal lament. Jonathan's love for the speaker David is a memory – in the past tense; David's distress will be ever present.

In 'Dirge for two Veterans', the American poet Walt Whitman (1819–1892) presents the death of a father and son during the Civil War as an American version of Saul and Jonathan:

For the son is brought with the father,
In the foremost ranks of the fierce assault they fell,
Two veterans, son and father, dropped together,
And the double grave awaits them.

And his lyric 'Reconciliation' (1881) conveys something of the sorrow David might have felt:

> Word over all, beautiful as the sky,
> Beautiful that war and all its deeds of carnage must in time be utterly lost,
> That the hands of the sisters Death and Night incessantly softly
> Wash again, and ever again, this soil'd world;
> For my enemy is dead, a man as divine as myself is dead,
> I look where he lies white-faced and still in the coffin – I draw near,
> Bend down and touch lightly with my lips the white face in the coffin.

Note the symmetry between the overarching sky, the 'Word over all' and the kiss that the speaker gently bestows on his enemy.

▶ How does the speaker communicate grief? In what ways does this poem draw on the language of David's lament?

George Eliot ends her novel *The Mill on the Floss* (1860) with the sentence 'In their death they were not divided.' This is written on the tombstone of the drowned brother and sister, Maggie and Tom Tulliver, who 'had gone down in an embrace never to be parted'. Thus George Eliot implies that love is present at the very moment of death, whereas Whitman's poem implies that death confers a universal brotherhood on man.

▶ What examples of close male friendship in the time of war can you find which echo the David and Jonathan story? For example, consider the relationship between Stephen and Jack in Sebastian Faulks' *Birdsong* or Owen and Sassoon in Pat Barker's *Regeneration*.

The *Song of Songs*

Also known as the *Song of Solomon*, this Old Testament book reads as a collection of love poems where God is never mentioned. It has been interpreted allegorically first as the relationship between God and Israel, and then between Christ and his Church. The collection can stand alone as an ecstatic celebration of the joy of passionate human love. (See the extract in Part 3, page 80.) In describing each other, the bridegroom and his bride repeatedly use the **blazon**, later seen in Petrarchan poetry:

> Behold, thou art fair, my love: behold thou are fair, thou hast doves' eyes within thy locks.
> Thy lips are like a thread of scarlet, and thy speech is comely: thy temples are like a piece of pomegranate within thy locks.
> Thy two breasts are like two young roes that are twins, which feed among the lilies.
>   ('The Bride', 4,vv.1 and 3)

His hands are as gold rings set with the beryl: his belly is as bright ivory overlaid with sapphires. His legs are as pillars of marble, set upon sockets of fine gold.

('The Bridegroom', 5 vv.14–15)

The lovers are about to make love. The eroticism is provocative:

My beloved put in his hand by the hole of the door, and my bowels were moved for him. I rose up to open to my beloved; and my hands dropped with myrrh, and my fingers with sweet smelling myrrh, upon the handles of the lock. I opened to my beloved; but my beloved had withdrawn himself and was gone: my soul failed when he spake …

(5 vv.4–6)

Desire is aroused by being deferred. The joy of lovemaking is celebrated: 'His left hand should be under my head, and his right hand should embrace me.' Every sense is awakened; the beloved is 'perfumed with wine and frankincense … the voice of the turtle dove is heard in the land: Thy lips, oh my spouse, drop as the honeycomb; honey and milk are under thy tongue.' Finally, the writer acknowledges that love will transcend death. 'Set me as a seal upon thine heart, as a seal upon thy arm, for love is as strong as death. Many waters cannot quench love, neither can the floods drown it.'

Many writers, including Shakespeare, George Herbert, Swinburne, Robert Graves and D.H. Lawrence in *Lady Chatterley's Lover*, have been influenced by the *Song of Songs*.

▶ Compare the blazon of the male beloved in *Song of Songs* with Cleopatra's description of her beloved Antony in *Antony and Cleopatra* (see Part 5, page 116). What is the effect of Cleopatra's hyperbole? Is either passage realistic?

The New Testament

The four Gospels in the New Testament narrate the life, death and resurrection of Jesus Christ. In St John's Gospel, Christ gives a new commandment, to replace the Ten Commandments of the Old Testament: 'This is my commandment, that ye love one another, as I have loved you. Greater love hath no man than this, that a man lay down his life for his friends' (John 15, vv.12–13). Some of Christ's parables paint pictures of this selfless and self-giving love, or *agape*. The Good Samaritan tends the injured traveller, left beaten and dying at the side of the road; the father rejoices at the return of the Prodigal Son, who had squandered his inheritance, ending up homeless and destitute, before returning to his family to ask forgiveness. The image of the Good Shepherd, who is prepared to lay down his life for his sheep, is used to describe Christ's love for his people.

The Virgin Mary

Mary is the mother of Jesus. St Luke's Gospel describes how she becomes pregnant, conceiving through the power of the Holy Spirit: 'And behold, thou shalt conceive in thy womb, and bring forth a son.' The moment when the divine becomes human is called the Incarnation – literally, the putting on of flesh. This mystery is given poetic form in this medieval lyric:

> He cam also stille
> To his mother's bower
> As dew in April
> That falleth on the flower.

The 'stille'ness evokes awe at the miraculous silent conception. The image of the 'dew in April', as well as approximating chronologically to the time of the Annunciation and the beginning of Mary's pregnancy, also suggests the renewal of spring. 'Dew' typologically is Christ, 'the flower' Mary.

Mary's tender devotion to the Christ Child has been represented in art from medieval times onwards. The Madonna cherishes the baby Jesus in her arms, in the stable in Bethlehem. Michelangelo sculpted the Pietà, to be seen in St Peter's Rome, a harrowing depiction of Mary cradling the dead body of her son after his corpse had been brought down from the Cross. Types or symbols of Mary in medieval poetry and art include the fountain, the door, the lily among thorns, the rose without a thorn, the star of the sea, the enclosed garden and, wonderfully, the chaste virgin, the tamer of the unicorn. The *Song of Songs* (see page 14, above) provides sources for much of this imagery.

In *The Glass Menagerie* (1944) American playwright Tennessee Williams uses 'the lovely fragility of glass' to represent the virginal innocence of the vulnerable Laura, who is associated in several ways with Mary. In his production notes Williams writes: 'The light on Laura should be distinct from the others, having a peculiar pristine clarity such as light used in early religious saints or madonnas.'

Like Mary, the unicorn tamer, Laura cherishes her miraculous glass unicorn, her pride and joy. And at the conclusion of the play, her brother Tom's words remind the audience of Laura's haunting innocence:

> I pass the lighted window of a shop where perfume is sold. The
> window is filled with pieces of colored glass, tiny transparent bottles
> in delicate colors, like bits of a shattered rainbow. Then all at once my
> sister touches my shoulder. I turn around and look into her eyes. Oh,
> Laura, Laura, I tried to leave you behind me, but I am more faithful
> than I intended to be! I reach for a cigarette, I cross the street, I run
> into the movies or a bar, I buy a drink, I speak to the nearest stranger
> – anything that can blow your candles out!
> [*Laura bends over the candles*]

For nowadays the world is lit by lightning! Blow out your candles, Laura – and so goodbye …
[*She blows the candles out.*]

▶ What is the effect of the religious imagery? How does the writer equate Laura with the Virgin Mary?

Mary Magdalene

Mary Magdalene appears in the New Testament as a follower of Christ, after he cast out her evil demons. She has been conflated with the Biblical woman taken in adultery who, in penitence, washed Jesus' feet with her hair and whose sins were forgiven. Certainly Mary was present at the foot of the Cross, attended the burial, and most significantly was the first to encounter the Risen Christ on Easter Morning. The painting by Titian, *Noli Me Tangere* ('Do Not Touch Me', 1514), in the National Gallery, depicts this encounter. The painting is full of reciprocal desire. Christ leans tenderly towards Mary Magdalene, who is kneeling on the ground. Mary yearns to touch Christ who has 'not yet risen to My Father'. Desire is appropriate if it has its proper object, which in this story must be God. This passionate desire for God is seen in the writings of medieval mystics such as Richard Rolle (1300–1349) and Julian of Norwich (1343–1413):

> Christ is our clothing. In his love he wraps and holds us. He enfolds us for love, and he will never let us go.
>
> (Julian of Norwich *Revelations of Divine Love*)

Michèle Roberts' novel *The Wild Girl* (1984) is a fictional account of an imagined relationship between Mary Magdalene and Christ. The metaphysical poet Richard Crashaw (1612–1649) depicted the sorrows of Mary in his poem, 'St Mary Magdalene, or the Weeper'. The extravagant metaphysical conceits which preface the poem are typical of his baroque, emotional style:

> Lo, where a Wounded Heart with bleeding Eyes conspire,
> Is she a Flaming fountain, or a weeping fire?

Ovid

Two thousand years ago, the Roman poet Ovid was banished from the centre of his world, Rome, to an obscure outpost of the Roman Empire, Tomis, on the Black Sea. Ovid always yearned to return to Rome but he died in exile, ten years later in AD 18.

Ovid's love poetry may be categorised according to genre: the *Amores*, or love **elegies**; the *Heroides*, verse letters; the didactic sex guide *Ars Amatoria*, and his epic poem, *Metamorphoses*. He has been described as 'Rome's great expert on love'.

Amores and *Heroides*

Ovid began to compose the *Amores* around BC 25. They chart the poet's developing relationship with his girl Corinna, from falling in love, through the highs and lows of passion, to break-up and the end of the affair. No topic is off limits: Corinna's botched abortion, sexual impotence on the poet's part, 'the imperfect enjoyment', irritation with the intrusive dawn, the joy of lovemaking on a sleepy Roman afternoon.

Elegy 1.5, 'Ovid's mistress comes to him at siesta time', has been variously translated by Christopher Marlowe (1564–1593), Richard Duke (1658–1711) and modern classical scholars, including Peter Green. Compare the openings of their three translations:

> In summer's heat and mid-time of the day
> To rest my limbs upon a bed I lay …   (Marlowe)

> 'Twas noon, when I, scorched with the double fire
> Of the hot sun and my more hot desire …   (Duke)

> A hot afternoon: siesta-time. Exhausted,
> I lay sprawled across my bed …   (Green)

▶ What questions do these contrasting translations prompt you to ask? Look particularly at the ***zeugma*** in the Duke translation.

The *Amores*, a comparatively early work, already displays features of Ovid's later writing: mood swings from flippancy to seriousness, cynicism, and a habit of puncturing moments of emotion with references to gods, mythological and legendary figures. Ovid involves his reader fully, through knowing asides. By contrast, the *Heroides* ('Epistles of the Heroines') are letters written by famous mythological women to their lovers. Helen writes to Paris, disingenuously complaining that she is unpractised in 'the art of love'. The abandoned Ariadne, having provided Theseus with the means of escape from the Minotaur in the labyrinth in Crete, laments her loss as she paces the shore on Naxos:

> By the moon's light I the wide shore did view,
> But all was desert, and no sign of you.
> Then every way with love's mad haste I fly,
> But ill my feet with my desires comply …
> (10: Ariadne to Theseus, translated by Lord Somers)

In *A Midsummer Night's Dream* by William Shakespeare (1595) Helena pursues her lover Demetrius through the wood: driven by 'love's mad haste' she utters a similar complaint, deploring her fate:

> I am your spaniel; and, Demetrius,
> The more you beat me I will fawn on you.

Use me but as your spaniel: spurn me, strike me,
Neglect me, lose me; only give me leave,
Unworthy as I am, to follow you.   (II.i.203–205)

The forsaken and rejected woman is a common feature in the literature of love.
Unlike Helena, whose distress takes the form of perpetual motion (for example,
'Enter running'), both Miss Havisham in *Great Expectations* (1861) and Mariana
in Tennyson's poem and Shakespeare's *Measure for Measure* (1604) are presented
as static, frozen by loss. Indeed Viola in *Twelfth Night* (1601) speaks of the unloved
emblematically as 'Patience on a monument / Smiling at Grief'.

▶ Consider the extract from *Eloisa to Abelard* (Part 3, page 82), an heroic epistle by
Alexander Pope. How does Pope convey Eloisa's continuing passion for Abelard? In
what ways does Pope's poem echo Ovid's *Heroides*?

Ars Amatoria

Ovid's most controversial work was his *Ars Amatoria*, or 'The Art of Love'. For
'love' read sexual seduction. This instructive sex guide was banished from Rome's
public libraries on the order of the Emperor Augustus, who was attempting to
raise the moral tone of the capital by outlawing adultery through legal decree. The
first two books are addressed to men, with the final book offering practical advice
to women on how to get and keep their man. To become a good lover, the *Ars
Amatoria* explains, requires cunning, effort and some expenditure. Local Roman
colour – references to the baths, the races, the amphitheatre – is interwoven with
mythic examples. Sardonic humour predominates and, as in the *Amores*, Ovid
adopts a pose of amused complicity with his reader. We will become the stuff of
legend ourselves if we imitate the famous. Rome has its very own celebrity culture.
If we learn to sing, we will become as seductive as the Sirens. However, a feeling of
genuine sorrow at the passage of time appears at the beginning of Book 3, where he
warns the young girls to make the most of their youth, **carpe diem**:

Have fun while you can, in your salad days; the years glide
Past like a moving stream,
And the water that's gone can never be recovered,
The lost hour never returns ...
There'll come a time
when
You who today lock out your lovers will lie
Old and cold and alone in bed, your door never broken
Open at brawling midnight, never at dawn
Scattered roses bright on your threshold!

(translated by Peter Green)

▶ Consider Robert Herrick's treatment of the *carpe diem* theme in 'To the Virgins, to Make Much of Time' (Part 3, page 83). How much does his imagery of flowers owe to Ovid?

The *Ars Amatoria* has influenced writers as various as Donne, Byron, Oscar Wilde and Vladimir Nabokov. It is also the precursor to a host of self-help 'love' manuals. John Gray's *Men are from Mars, Women are from Venus* (1992) is indebted to Ovid from the title onwards.

Metamorphoses

Ovid wrote his *Metamorphoses* about 2000 years ago. It is vast in scope, with the stories ranging from before the world was created to Ovid's future projected immortality: 'Now I shall live in fame.' Every well-known Greek and Roman myth plays its part in Ovid's epic poem, the common link being that of transformation. The *Metamorphoses* has been a central text in European literature, attracting playwrights and poets from the Renaissance to the present day. Former Poet Laureate, Ted Hughes (1930–1998), produced a much praised translation of the poems shortly before his death.

In the *Metamorphoses* Love, as Ovid seeks to demonstrate, drives us to the very edge, to extremes of passion. We literally become 'ecstatic', standing outside the body. The human frame bursts its boundaries and morphs into the natural world. Ovid recounts how Daphne, pursued by the god Apollo, becomes a laurel tree; how the beautiful huntress Callisto, seduced and made pregnant by Jupiter, king of the gods, undergoes a double transformation – first, shamefully, into a hairy bear by the vengeful Juno, wife and sister of Jupiter, then into the double constellation, the Great and Small Bear, with her son.

Two tales from *Metamorphoses* have particularly influenced the literature of love: Echo and Narcissus, and Pygmalion and Galatea.

Echo and Narcissus

This story is contained in Book 3. Echo, a nymph, saw Narcissus out hunting, and instantly fell in love with his astonishing beauty. Previously cursed by Juno into repeating the last words of others, Echo was not able to express her passion for Narcissus. She pined after him, but he brutally rejected her.

> Love was fixed in her body
> Like a barbed arrow. There it festered
> With his rejection.

Her beauty faded, the flesh fell from her body, she became voice and bone and her bones became stone. Only her voice, the echo, was left. Narcissus continued to rebuff his many admirers. One day he lay down at the side of a tranquil pool to quench his thirst. Transfixed by the exquisitely beautiful youth he saw in the water, he attempted in vain to embrace him.

> Falling deeper and deeper in love
> With what so many had loved so hopelessly.
> Not recognising himself
> He wanted only himself.
> … He was himself
> The torturer who now began his torture.   (Ted Hughes)

Utterly unable to bear the torment of self-love, Narcissus melted away, destroyed by the flame of passion. His body was never found – only 'a flower with a trumpet of gold and pale yellow flowers' – the narcissus.

This story raises interesting questions about the nature of love and identity. Narcissus is consumed by love of his own self, Echo is destroyed through her love for another. Her whole existence, even her voice, is dependent on the other. When Narcissus rejects her she fades away to a disembodied echo. Excessive self-love is now known as narcissism. In *Twelfth Night* (1601) Olivia accuses Malvolio of being 'sick of self love'. W.H. Auden, in his poem 'Alone' (Part 3, page 83), explores the tension between imagined love and reality. What does this poem suggest about the relationship between love and isolation?

Pygmalion and Galatea

This story occurs in Book 10. Pygmalion was a sculptor living alone on Cyprus. Shocked by the sinfulness of women around him, he resolved to sculpt his own perfect woman. He made a woman 'lovelier than any living woman'. He fell in love with his creation, worshipping, kissing, stroking and caressing the statue as if it were alive. On the day of the festival of Venus, he laid his offerings to the goddess of love on her altar. His fervent prayer was to wed a woman like his ivory carving. To his utter astonishment and joy, his request was granted. Cool ivory became warm flesh.

> She woke to his kisses and blushed
> To find herself kissing
> One who kissed her,
> And opened her eyes for the first time
> To the light and her lover together.   (Ted Hughes)

This story illustrates the transforming power of love. It is a metamorphosis in reverse. Here stone becomes flesh. As in the fairy tale, *Sleeping Beauty*, the dormant beloved is awoken by a kiss. *The Winter's Tale* by Shakespeare (1610) ends with a scene of resurrection. Hermione, presumed dead, is presented as a statue to her repentant husband Leontes. With ceremonial grace, the statue becomes a living woman. The playwright George Bernard Shaw refashioned the Pygmalion myth in his play *Pygmalion* (1916), which was later adapted into the musical *My Fair Lady*.

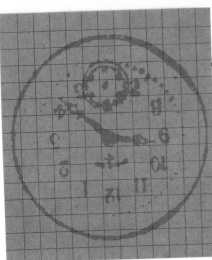

n transformation, the dancer Isadora Duncan
counts the occasion when she met the sculptor
veen sculpting and the female body in her language:

red lids, his eyes blazing, and then, with the
ad before his works, he came towards me.
neck, breast, stroked my arms and ran his
e legs and feet. He began to knead my
ay.

(Isadora Duncan *My Life*, 1927)

vith the Pygmalion myth? What is the effect of
object of desire?

Courtly love

Courtly love, or *fin amor*, began in Provence in the 12th century, and spread
through the courts of Northern France, Italy and Germany. An aristocratic
pastime, lovers became members of the 'court of love', with its special rituals
and routines. Andreas Capellanus, a monk at the court of Countess Marie of
Champagne, even codified the rules of love in *De Arte Honeste Amandi (On The Art
of Honourable Loving)*. At the same time, a whole language of love was created by
the troubadours.

In many ways, courtly love is remarkably similar to modern notions of romantic
love. The lover falls passionately in love at first sight with the beloved. He suffers
the pangs of love, wishing to be worthy of the beloved. He may have to overcome
obstacles to gain her love. Often the love affair, if adulterous, has to be kept secret.
But there are important differences, so it is instructive to consider the sources
and literature of courtly love, before examining the radical way in which Chaucer
revolutionised the concept, parodying it through *fabliaux* and exposing its more
disturbing elements.

Troudabours

Troubadours were accomplished Provençal poets of the 12th and 13th century,
influential in the development of love poetry. They often acquired celebrity status:
the troubadour Peire Vidal took his adoration of a lady named La Loba (the wolf)
to extremes, dressing up in wolf skins in order to be hunted over the mountains
by shepherds. Troubadours were musicians too: their lyrics were set to music, and
they travelled from court to court performing their songs from memory. Significant
features of their poetry included a religious adoration of the lady and the cult of joy,
or *jois,* from love. The jealous husband and the talebearer also became stock figures.
The practices of *fin amor* were refined. It was as important to create a beautifully
crafted poem as it was to express undying love for the beloved. In one lyric

Arnaut Daniel (1180–1200), regarded as the ultimate love poet by both Dante and Petrarch, as well as by the 20th-century poets T.S. Eliot and Ezra Pound, writes:

> In this little song, pretty and gay, I compose words, I plane and polish them, so that they will be true and certain when I have passed the file over them. For Love immediately smoothes and gilds my singing, which originates from her who possesses and controls deserving.

The troubadour is a craftsman, who refines language in the same way a carpenter planes wood. Love, *Amor*, is personified, always feminine in troubadour poetry, radiantly enhancing the sweet lyricism of his song. But Daniel's final two stanzas are different in tone:

> I do not at all cease to love nobly because of the pain I suffer, although it keeps me in the wilderness. And so out of it I make these words in verse: as a lover I suffer worse than the man who labours ...

> I am Arnaut who loves the wind and hunts the hare from the ox's back and who swims against the rising tide.

Here, *fin amor* is not social. He is excluded, kept 'in the wilderness'. He endures pain, indeed the pain propels him to poetry. The final stanza expresses the madness of love. His world is the wilderness: the civilising sweetness of his little love song vanishes in his elemental energy. This remarkable poem explodes any clichés of courtly love. Love which disturbs and maddens also occurs in texts such as *Wuthering Heights* and *Othello*. (See Part 2, 'Love as a madness', pages 39–40.)

Le Roman de la Rose

> And if any man or woman should ask what I wish this romance to be called, it is the *Romance of the Rose* in which the whole art of love is contained.

Written in two uneven parts, by two different authors, separated by almost fifty years, *Le Roman de la Rose* is a key text of courtly love and was a bestseller. The first 4058 lines were written by Guillaume de Lorris in 1230. Jeun de Meun completed the poem in 1275, adding over 17,000 lines. Chaucer himself translated the first section, and certainly many features of this courtly love allegory appear in his writings on love: the dream vision (particularly 'The Book of the Duchess'), the May morning setting, and the naive narrator.

As in the *Ars Amatoria* and *De Amore*, love has its rules and its philosophy. The plot of *Le Roman de la Rose* is simple. A young man falls asleep. He dreams a wonderful dream in which he enters a heavenly spring garden and discovers the spring of love, where Narcissus (see page 20, above) had died. At the bottom of the spring lie two crystals, which reflect the whole of the garden. However, Love has ensnared him. He who gazes at his own reflection, as Narcissus did, will fall passionately in love with the next thing he sees. He sees rose bushes growing abundantly, and chooses a beautiful bud, fragrant and perfect. The god of love shoots the following five arrows directly at him: Beauty, Simplicity, Courtesy, Company and Fair Seeming. The arrowheads lodge in his breast, and he suffers delicious pain.

> Now you may know for certain that if I had greatly desired the rose-bud before, my longing was also increased, and as the pain grew more intense, so did my desire continually to approach the little rose that smelt sweeter than violets.

He swears allegiance to the god of Love, who in return honours him with the commandments, which he gives to true lovers. Lovers will endure agonies of suffering, but be comforted by Hope. Love also gives three other gifts as consolation to the suffering lover: Pleasant Thought, Pleasant Conversation and Pleasant Looks. The story continues as the narrator meets various allegorical figures who either help him to approach the rose, or angrily turn him away from his heart's desire.

The lengthy second section, written by Jeun de Meun, is a philosophical account of love. Reason provides an extended **oxymoronic** sermon:

> Love is hostile peace and loving hatred, disloyal loyalty and loyal disloyalty; it is confident fear and desperate hope, demented reason and reasonable madness … a healthful sickness and a most sickly health … a hell that soothes and a heaven that tortures, a prison that offers relief to prisoners, a cold and wintry spring time.

Disorientated by the stream of contradictions, the narrator claims to learn nothing from it!

▶ Compare this extract with Romeo's complaint to Benvolio, in the first Act of *Romeo and Juliet*. What similarities can you detect?

▶ Consider 'Song of Troilus' (Part 3, page 84). Troilus has fallen in love with the beautiful Crisyede, and is cherishing the memory of her image, alone in his room. He resolves to compose a lament. How does what he says here about the paradoxical nature of love relate to Jean de Meun's sermon in *Le Roman de la Rose*?

Features of courtly love

Courtly love presents the process of falling in love formally.

The first feature is love at first sight. The stimulus to love is always from an external source. The lover is a passive recipient of an external stimulus, usually visual. The process is twofold. The lover beholds someone whom he then proceeds to desire greatly. Love comes in through the eyes and makes its home in the heart. This moment has been likened to a piercing fleshly wound. The lover has been shafted by an arrow from the god of love. Guillaume de Lorris describes this stage by stage in *Le Roman de la Rose*:

> The point entered my eye and penetrated my heart. I immediately fell backwards. My heart was false and failed me and I lay a long time in a swoon. When I recovered consciousness and came to my senses I was very weak and therefore imagined that I had lost a lot of blood. But the point that pierced me drew no blood at all and the wound was quite dry.

The psychological disorientation, presenting as a physical injury, is medically described. On catching sight of the fair Emelye walking in the garden below, Palamon (in Chaucer's *Knight's Tale*) exclaims:

> I was hurt now right thrughout myn ye,
> into myn herte, that wol my bane be.

Another feature of courtly love is love as a sickness: the lover will suffer both physically and mentally. Love is its own sickness and its own remedy (see Part 2, page 43). The famous romance of Tristan and Isolde (by Gottfried von Strassburg, d. 1210) tells of love, sexual passion and consuming death. Their love is inflamed through drinking a love potion on board a ship. Here, the patients heal themselves through the ministrations of Love, or more simply, through making love:

> That night, as the lovely woman lay brooding and pining for her darling, there came stealing into her cabin her lover and her physician – Tristan and Love. Love the physician led Tristan, her sick one, by the hand: there too, she found her other patient Isolde. She quickly took both sufferers, and gave him to her, her to him, to be each other's remedy.

Secrecy, too, is important. 'Love that is made public rarely lasts,' warns Andreas Capellanus. Lovers' trysts must take place in private: a secluded garden of love (the *hortus conclusus*) or, as here, the ship's cabin. The affair may be adulterous, therefore secrecy is essential.

Chaucer

In *The Canterbury Tales* and *Troilus and Criseyde*, Chaucer recounts with both compassion and humour the sufferings of the courtly lover. How does the lover pursue the beloved? In order to gain the love of the beloved, the lover must not only be prepared to endure physical and psychological suffering, but must undergo many trials. This is in the tradition of *fin amor*.

In the *Knight's Tale* the two knights, Palamon and Arcite, are imprisoned, exiled and fight to the death to win the hand of the fair Emilye. Arcite suffers torments, becoming a skeletal wraith. It is no accident that he is described as becoming as thin and dry as an arrow, the very metaphorical instrument of his torture:

> So much sorwe hadde nevere creature
> That is, or shal, whyl that the world may dure,
> His sleep, his mete, his drink is him iraft,
> That len he wex and drye as is a shaft.
> His eyen holwe, and grisly to biholde;
> His hewe fallow and pale as ashen colde;
> And solitarie he was and evere alone,
> And wailinge al the night, making his mone.

In *The Franklin's Tale* Chaucer brings affectionate humour to his description of the married Dorigen's admirer, Aurelius, who pines for her and

> Languissheth as a furie dooth in helle;
> And dye he moste, he seyde, as dide Echo
> For Narcissus, that dorste nat telle her wo.

The irony comes in the narrator's passing comment, 'he seyde' ensuring that we don't take Aurelius' protestations too seriously. Unlike Echo, he *is* able to express his lovelorn misery in various forms of nicely crafted lyrics, 'songs, compleintes, roundels and virelayes'.

Fabliaux: Chaucer and the comedy of love

Chaucer was adept at parodying, or sending up, the whole concept of courtly love in the *fabliaux* within *The Canterbury Tales*. Originally, *fabliaux* were short comic French narratives, of around 600 lines. Cheerfully immoral, characters usually achieve their ends through low-level cunning and manipulation of those around them. In *The Merchant's Tale,* Januarie, the aged, possessive husband, is **cuckolded** by Damyon, the young squire. Humour arises through farce, through the distortion of courtly love values and the misappropriation of Biblical texts. For instance, the Miller's wife, Alison, is serenaded under her window by Absalon, the parish clerk, in his version of the *Song of Songs*:

> What do ye, hony-comb, swete Alisoun
> My faire brid, my swete cinamone?

Probably *fabliaux* are best known for their scatological and graphically sexual elements. Farts, pudenda kissed in error, branded buttocks, love letters dropped down lavatories and sex in a pear tree are all crucial plot devices in *The Miller's Tale* and *The Merchant's Tale*.

Petrarch

Francesco Petrarca (1304–1374) was a distinguished Italian poet and humanist. Born in Arezzo, he travelled widely as a papal and diplomatic envoy. Petrarch was also a great classical scholar, who did much to revive interest in the study of ancient Greek and Latin literature. The great triumph of his life was to be crowned Poet Laureate on the Capitol in Rome on Easter Sunday 1341. Today, Petrarch is best known for his *Canzoniere* or *rime sparse* (scattered rhyme), an extended sonnet sequence inspired by and dedicated to his beloved Laura.

Laura and the *rime sparse*

To some critics, Laura is a fiction. To others she had a real identity and was possibly even an ancestor of the Marquis de Sade. What is certain is that Petrarch noted, in the flyleaf of his pocket Virgil, the momentous day and time when he first cast eyes on her:

> Laura, illustrious through her own virtues, and long famed through my verses, first appeared to my eyes in my youth, in the year of our Lord 1327, on the sixth day of April, in the church of St. Clare in Avignon, at matins; and in the same city, also on the sixth day of April, at the same first hour, but in the year 1348, the light of her life was withdrawn from the light of day, while I, as it chanced, was in Verona, unaware of my fate.
>
> (translated by E.H. Wilkins, in *Life of Petrarch*, 1961)

To Petrarch, both these dates were of immense significance. According to the book of Genesis, God had created man on the sixth day. The 6th of April 1327 was the anniversary of Christ's crucifixion, Good Friday: 'It was the day when the sun's rays turned pale with grief for his Maker when I was taken.' (Petrarch, Sonnet 3). Easter Day, 6th April 1348, was the date of Laura's death. Therefore, she becomes an intimate part of the cycle of death and resurrection. Her immortality is assured as Petrarch keeps her alive through his poetry.

Petrarch, the poet, is Apollo, smitten with the golden arrows of desire, and burning with the fires of passion. Laura is the disdainful lady, Daphne, who never returns the poet's love. The poet never consummates his love. In Sonnet 6 the poet writes:

> … so far astray is my mad desire, in pursuing her who has turned in flight, and light, and free of the snares of Love, flies ahead of my slow running.

He is also Apollo the poet who will immortalise or transform his beloved Laura through his song, his *Canzoniere*. He too will be garlanded with praise for his poetic triumph. Her name shimmers with linguistic possibility, at once *l'aura* – the dawn – and noble tree, garland, honoured branch and, as we have seen, most poignantly, the wind, as at her death 'the wind carried off the words' (Sonnet 267).

Petrarch's love for Laura stands within the troubadour tradition, particularly the *rime petrose* of Arnaut Daniel (stony rhymes, so called because of the hard-hearted lady, see page 23, above), where the poet adores from afar the beautiful lady utterly beyond his reach, worshipping her as an earthly representation of God's divine grace. 'From her comes the courageous joy that leads you to heaven along a straight path, so that already I go high with hope.' (Sonnet 13). As we have seen, Petrarch was writing within a religious or theological context. He defined love in two ways. The first love is *caritas*, which is a divine love, a love for that which God has created; the second love is *cupiditas*, a love which enjoys something for its own sake. Both loves have their place. After Laura's death, Petrarch was able to love her purely for her spiritual goodness. Whilst she was alive, Petrarch at times felt that his obsessive love for Laura was sinful.

Petrarchan features to identify

It is worth considering Sonnet 61 in full (the following prose translation is by Robert Durling):

> Blessed be the day and the month and the year and the season and the time and the hour and the instant and the beautiful countryside and the place where I was struck by the two lovely eyes that have bound me;
> And blessed be the first sweet trouble I felt on being made one with Love, and the bow and the arrows that pierced me, and the wounds that reach my heart!
> Blessed be the many words I have scattered calling the name of my lady, and the sighs and the tears and the desire;
> And blessed be all the pages where I gain fame for her, and my thoughts, which are only of her, so no other has part in them!

Here, the word 'blessed' reverberates through the poem, uniting and sanctifying the time, the place, the action, the wounding by Love (*Amor*) and the poetry itself – the scattered words or *rima sparse*. Petrarch was to view Laura's dark eyes as the window to the soul, and the body as a veil, concealing the soul. His love for her has been interpreted as a Platonic love in which the lover willingly endures pain: the oxymoronic 'sweet trouble'. Ironically, only she who wounds has the power to heal: 'the lovely eyes struck me in such a way that they themselves could heal the wound'. The lover aches to hold and possess the beloved. He is utterly at her mercy. She may bestow grace upon him, by treating him kindly, or she may simply reject him. Finally, in this poem there is a reference to the *rima sparse*. Like

Arnaut Daniel, the troubadour (see page 23, above), Petrarch is aware of his status as a master-craftsman, a poet. He may immortalise his Laura through the written words of his poetry, but his own immortality is assured too.

Petrarch's influence on the literature of love

Petrarch wrote his sonnet sequence in the vernacular, in his native Italian rather than Latin. He developed courtly love into an art form by his creation of a sonnet sequence, exploring the range of emotions the anguished lover experiences and also celebrating the physical and spiritual qualities of the idealised beloved.

He also gave his name to the 'Petrarchan' sonnet, a fourteen-line poem in two parts. The first eight lines are known as the octave, usually rhyming abba, abba, and the final six lines are the sestet, usually cde, cde. The break between the octave and the sestet is known as the *volta* or turn, indicating a change in tone or mood. The limited rhyme heightens the intensity of the passion felt for the beloved.

Petrarch used the extended conceit to structure his poetry. One sonnet speaks metaphorically of the lover as a ship driven towards an impending doom; the waves, the rocks, and the driving wind all feature. This may be compared to Romeo's final soliloquy as he impetuously embraces his destiny:

> Thou desperate pilot, now at once run on
> The dashing rocks thy seasick weary bark!
> Here's to my love … Thus with a kiss I die.   (V.iii.116–120)

Petrarch's imagery is often extreme, or hyperbolic. When he weeps, his eyes become fountains. On seeing Laura swimming naked, he writes:

> She made me, even now, when the sky is burning, tremble with the chill of love.

Passionate emotions are defined in terms of the elements: 'wind of sighs', 'fire of torments'. The lover has been wounded by *Amor*, the god of love, shooting his arrows from the beloved's eyes; therefore, military imagery – the bow and arrow, the battle, the siege, and the fortress – appears regularly and provides a firmly defined oxymoronic base to the sonnet sequence. How can love and warfare co-exist? How can 'lovely eyes' assault or even kill? Petrarch defines the process with logical precision:

> Thus you, lady, felt the shot from your eyes pass straight through my inward parts, wherefore my heart must overflow through the wound with eternal tears.

Laura is his 'sweet fortress'. She herself, like Daphne, will never be aroused or penetrated by Love's golden arrow. She remains virginal and inviolate. He celebrates her ideal beauty through the blazon. Mercutio in *Romeo and Juliet* parodies this, putting an obscene slant on the convention. He is trying to raise the absent Romeo:

> I conjure thee by Rosaline's bright eyes,
> By her high forehead and her scarlet lip,
> By her fine foot, straight leg, and quivering thigh,
> And the demesnes that there adjacent lie,
> That in thy likeness thou appear to us.　　　　　　(II.i.17–21)

Classical imagery, from Ovid's *Metamorphoses*, is present. Laura, the icy lady, is Narcissus, self-loving and self-absorbed. The poet calls in vain, like Echo, but as we have seen, the 'wind carried away the words'. He envies Pygmalion who, unlike him, eventually possessed and cherished the warm, living flesh of the former statue. Bernini, the Roman artist, fascinated by the legend of Apollo and Daphne, sculpted the very moment of possession, transfiguration and metamorphosis. (This sculpture is in the Villa Borghese in Rome.) Prematurely crowned with laurel, Apollo embraces the trunk of the beautiful Daphne, whose upraised arms and fingers are sprouting leaves and tendrils.

Finally, Love or *Amor* is an ever-present figure. He is the recipient of the poet's complaints. An excellent marksman, he shoots his arrows with terrifying precision. There is no sense at all that he is Cupid, a charming little cherub, as will be seen later in the poetry of Lady Mary Wroth (Part 3, page 85).

Assignments

1 What does Plato have to say about love as a madness? Compare Socrates' explanation of love as a madness with Duke Theseus' speech at the end of *A Midsummer Night's Dream* and any other relevant texts you have studied.

2 What do you consider to be the relationship between Shakespeare's early sonnets, where he implores the young man to marry and procreate so that he may pass on his beauty for future generations, and Diotima's Ascent of Love speech (page 9, above)?

3 How often have you come across imagery of wings and flight in your reading in the literature of love? What may they represent?

4 Note how often in literature the horse is a symbol of sexual passion. Consider the presentation of horses in texts such as Chaucer's *Reeve's Tale*, *The Rainbow* and *Women in Love* by D.H. Lawrence, *Equus* by Peter Shaffer. What does this suggest about the difference between female and male sexuality?

5 What aspects of courtly love survive in the love literature of the 21st century?

6 Compare the presentation of any doomed lovers with that of Adam and Eve. You may wish to compare passages within *Paradise Lost* (Part 3, page 79).

2 | Approaching the texts

- How do individual writers contribute to the development of the literature of love?

- What different types of love literature can be identified?

- What types of texts and genres constitute the literature of love?

How is passion and desire conveyed in the literature of love? In *Desire: Love Stories in Western Culture* (1994) the critic Catherine Belsey writes:

> Passion in romance is commonly a storm, a flood, a tidal wave, or sometimes flames, a volcano or an earthquake. In all these cases it is elemental, beyond control, majestic, thrilling, dangerous. The helpless protagonist experiences desire as burning, falling through space, submerging or drowning. Metaphors of desire repeatedly invoke not pleasure, but various kinds of natural disturbance or disaster.

Lovers create new worlds of love, transcending time and space. The lover yearns for the beloved; love is an insatiable appetite and every emotion experienced is heightened and extreme, 'elemental', but passion may drive those in its grip to a frenzy of madness, the demon lover embodying the dark side of desire. Transgressive and unrequited love are aspects of passion and desire which will be considered below.

The geography of love

In the literature of love, lovers enter new worlds. They 'find' each other. The body of the beloved may be discovered, explored and possessed. Lovers also create their own world, which may illuminate or stand apart from the world in which they exist. The American poet E.E. Cummings (1894–1962) in the poem 'somewhere I have never travelled, gladly beyond' (Part 3, page 85) compares the sensuous discovery of his lover's body to 'somewhere I have never travelled'. Paradoxically, the more ethereal the lover is, the more she overwhelms him with her physical presence:

> nothing which we are to perceive in this world equals
> the power of your intense fragility: whose texture
> compels me with the colour of its countries…

At once romantic and lyrical, with echoes of the blazon (eyes, fingers, hands) and the Romantic image of the rose at its heart, the poem still surprises. Tender synaesthesia helps to shape a new world: 'eyes have their silence', looks 'unclose', the 'voice of your eyes is deeper than all roses' and 'nobody, not even the rain, has such small hands'. Tennessee Williams used this last statement as the epigraph in *The Glass Menagerie*.

One of the most delicately erotic poems in the canon of love poetry is Tennyson's 'Now sleeps the crimson petal, now the white' from *The Princess* (1847). The form is loosely that of a *ghazal*, a Middle Eastern form of lyric love poetry in metrical couplets, with a repeated, insistently patterned rhyme. The princess is reading the poem to herself:

> Now lies the Earth all Danaë to the stars,
> And all thy heart lies open unto me.
>
> Now slides the silent meteor on, and leaves
> A shining furrow, as thy thoughts in me.
>
> Now folds the lily all her sweetness up,
> And slips into the bosom of the lake:
>
> So fold thyself, my dearest, thou, and slip
> Into my bosom, and be lost in me.

The landscape is languorously personified: flowers sleep and 'fold' into the 'bosom' of the lake. The earth is Danaë, ready to be ravished and penetrated by the stars, as Jupiter raped Danaë, disguised as a shower of gold. The speaker desires to make love to the beloved – to slide like a 'silent meteor' – and to hold his beloved in his bosom. A *ghazal* is a poem to be set to music, and the musical qualities of Tennyson's verse are apparent here, through the thematic repetition of simple words, 'now' and 'me' emphasising his desire. The moment is 'now', rhyming with 'thou' to be made complete with 'me'. It is as simple as that: perfect unity.

The speaker in John Donne's Elegy 19: 'To His Mistress Going to Bed' also wants to make love to his mistress, but his desire is urgent and insistent. Her clothes are dazzling and enticing, but her naked body, 'a far fairer world', is for the poet alone to enjoy. She is his 'new found land'. They are Adam and Eve in reverse, discovering a spiritual innocence in nudity:

> Full nakedness, all joys are due to thee.
> As souls unbodied, bodies unclothed must be,
> To taste whole joys.

The climax of the poem comes as Donne yearns to begin making love:

> License my roving hands, and let them go
> Before, behind, between, above, below.
> O my America! my new found land,
> My kingdom, safeliest when with one man manned,

My mine of precious stones, my empery,
How blessed am I in this discovering thee!
To enter in these bonds, is to be free;
Then where my hand is set, my seal shall be.

His hands are 'roving' but must be authorised, or 'licensed', giving an erotic charge to the poem. Without her consent, the actions defined in the second line by the string of alliterative prepositions would enact rape. However, the poet brings control precisely through the alliteration and the disyllables. Desire is expressed through geography. She is his 'America … new found land … kingdom … empery'. The specific grows in geographical and imperial grandeur as he enters her, and simultaneously the language acquires a religious dimension. He is 'blessed'; he enters into a covenant and imprints his seal. The imagery here is from the *Song of Songs* (see Part 1, page 14). The 'roving' hands are formalised and 'set' at the end as a seal of constancy.

▶ Why do you think that 'my' is repeated so many times? Do you consider Donne's Elegy 19 to be a 'male' poem?

By contrast with the metaphysical conceits of John Donne, a quirkily comic 'take' on the geography of love is to be found in James Fenton's 'In Paris with You' (1993). The speaker echoes Cole Porter's lyrics, 'Let's Do it, Let's Fall in Love'. Here are the first and last stanzas:

Don't talk to me of love. I've had an earful
And I get tearful when I've downed a drink or two.
I'm one of your talking wounded.
I'm a hostage. I'm maroonded.
But I'm in Paris with you.

Don't talk to me of love. Let's talk of Paris.
I'm in Paris with the slightest thing you do.
I'm in Paris with your eyes, your mouth,
I'm in Paris with … all points south.
Am I embarrassing you?
I'm in Paris with you.

The speaker adopts an intimately aggressive tone at first, masking subtle linguistic wordplay. The phrase 'talking wounded' is a 20th-century Petrarchan conceit, refashioning the image of love as a battle for the chattering classes. The final stanza is pure Donne. The anaphora 'I'm in Paris' followed in the second stanza by the ellipsis before 'all points south' give the reader's imagination licence to roam. Witty feminine (wounded / maroonded) and internal rhyme (earful / tearful) make this a poem to be read out loud.

Food and desire

So are you to my thoughts as food to life   (Shakespeare: Sonnet 75)

There has always been a relationship, in the literature of love, between eating and sex. Appetite, or desire, is present; indeed a desire to possess the body of another is termed a 'carnal' desire, from the Latin *carne*, meaning meat. Both involve physical processes: the sight of a feast may please, and appetite is subsequently aroused through smell and touch. The consumption of the feast itself gives further sensory pleasures. Finally appetite or desire is satisfied. But when desire is not met, or appetite gratified, such as in the courtly love tradition (see Part 1, page 22), the lover may pine away, refusing all food until the remote beloved bestows her favours upon him. After the death of a lover, the partner left behind on earth may choose to embrace a different kind of desire, a desire to unite with the lover through starvation. This is evident in *Wuthering Heights* in the ferocity of Heathcliff's desire to join Cathy beyond the grave (see below, page 41 and Part 3, page 87).

In Book 4 of Milton's *Paradise Lost* (1667) feasting and love-making are joyously celebratory aspects of life in Paradise. Satan, 'on the Tree of Life', sitting 'like a cormorant', views Adam and Eve going about their daily business. After a day of 'sweet gardening labour':

> to their supper fruits they fell,
> Nectarine fruits which the compliant boughs
> Yielded them, sidelong as they sat recline
> On the soft downy bank damasked with flowers:
> The savoury pulp they chew, and in the rind
> Still as they thirsted scoop the brimming stream;
> Nor gentle purpose, nor endearing smiles
> Wanted, nor youthful dalliance as beseems
> Fair couple, linked in happy nuptial league,
> Alone as they.

The passage contains references to the Golden Age. Man lives in harmony with nature. The boughs are 'compliant' in serving man's needs; the stream is 'brimming', eternally flowing with abundant water to slake his thirst. Adam and Eve recline upon the 'soft, downy bank damasked with flowers' – highly sensual writing, which could be a description of Eve's body, and which anticipates Lawrence's description of the love-making of Lady Chatterley and Mellors in *Lady Chatterley's Lover* (first published privately in 1928, the complete unexpurgated version published by Penguin in 1960 who were then prosecuted under the Obscene Publications Act). The symbiosis between man and nature leads into 'youthful dalliance', proper marital affection. Only the first six words of the above passage foreshadow the impending tragedy, culminating in the word 'fell'. 'Fruit' causes their downfall, but they fall 'together'.

But the hour of noon approaches. Eve, led to the Tree of Knowledge by the wily Satan disguised as the serpent, is excitingly aroused by the prospect of the forbidden fruit; every sense is awakened and she longs for the fruit just as Satan pined in 'longing' at the sight of Adam and Eve. (See Part 3, page 79.) Unsatisfied desire has now entered Paradise. When Eve bites the apple, Earth is personified as a woman groaning in childbirth, anticipating Eve's punishment for disobeying God by eating the apple from the Tree of Life. The passage begins and ends with speech, and Milton makes it clear through the syntax of his second sentence, and the use of qualifications such as 'as seemed' and 'fancied so' that language itself is unstable. Nothing will be as it seems from now onwards. Eve is utterly focused on the taste of the fruit. All her earlier decorum and moderation are lost and she is now in thrall to an insatiable appetite, which she has brought into Paradise. Moreover, she appears 'heightened as with wine': the Error of the Fall has often been compared with that of intoxication. There is an ugliness in her greed as evidenced by the alliteration. Instead of acquiring the god-like wisdom promised by Satan, she is ignorant as to what she has done: she 'knew not eating death'. This oxymoron 'eating death' is the climax of the passage. 'Eating' should sustain life, but here it has brought death into the world. Death has its own appetite and desires. Consider all the references to devouring death in *Romeo and Juliet* and *Antony and Cleopatra*; for example, 'Earth hath swallowed all my hopes but she.'

Finally **post-lapsarian** sex is of a very different nature compared with the innocent and moderate embraces of the unfallen Adam and Eve. Both are aroused sexually after eating the fruit and so desire to consume each other. Eve's eye 'darted contagious fire' (see the discussion of Petrarch's passion for Laura in Part 1, page 27). Unlike the **pre-lapsarian** love-making, there is very little foreplay, 'Her hand he seized'. The verb 'seized' has violent undertones. Does Adam dominate Eve, or is their lust mutual? The love-making is recorded in the lexis of appetite:

> There they took their fill of love and love's disport
> Took largely, of their mutual guilt the seal.

The act of sex itself becomes both an inverse sacrament of guilt, 'a seal' which unites the pair, and a means whereby they console each other, in a sinful world. Love-making is now debased to merely 'play', and the first post-coital sleep in the fallen world becomes an uneasy image of death.

Eve was tempted by forbidden fruit, seduced through food. This event is replayed, with variations, in three texts: 'The Eve of St Agnes' by Keats (1820), 'Goblin Market' by Christina Rossetti (1862) and *Atonement* by Ian McEwan (2001). In the 'The Eve of St Agnes' (a ballad much influenced by *Romeo and Juliet*) Porphyro, the young lover, steals into Madeline's bedchamber, watches her undress and prepares the following banquet for her:

> And still she slept an azure-lidded sleep,
> In blanched linen, smooth and lavendered,

> While he from forth the closet brought a heap
> Of candied apple, quince, and plum, and gourd,
> With jellies soother than the creamy curd,
> And lucent syrops, tinct with cinnamon;
> Manna and dates, in argosy transferred
> From Fez; and spiced dainties, every one,
> From silken Samarcand to cedared Lebanon.

The journeying of the fruits, first from the closet, then from the exotic East is a conjuring trick of luxurious abundance, the work of an illusionist, with a sophisticated feminine rhyme (cinnamon / every one / Lebanon) reflecting the overflowing profusion.

The poet creates a sensory tension in that the writing appeals to our sense of taste – it is not primarily visual, because of course Madeline is asleep, but we, as audience, stand on the outside of her dream, looking in at her 'azure' coloured eyelids. Her bedlinen is 'blanched,' symbolic of her virginity. What happens next may be suggested by Keats' fascination with the boundary between sleep and waking. He had marked in his own copy of *The Tempest* Caliban's words, 'when I waked / I cried to dream again'. Madeline awakes, thinks she has been dreaming of Porphyro and yearns for the Porphyro of her dreams, confessing her love for him, 'For if thou diest, my love, I know not where to go.' He responds accordingly:

> Beyond a mortal man impassioned far
> At these voluptuous accents, he arose,
> Ethereal, flush'd, and like a throbbing star
> Seen mid the sapphire heaven's deep repose;
> Into her dream he melted, as the rose
> Blendeth its odour with the violet,
> Solution sweet ...

▶ Keats once said that 'he did not want ladies to read his poetry'. How erotic do you find this writing? How effective is the sexual symbolism and early 19th-century diction to modern eyes and ears?

'Goblin Market' by Christina Rossetti (1860) relates the story of two sisters, Laura and Lizzie, who hear the siren call of the goblins in the mountain, selling fruit which they both know to be forbidden. Laura is tempted, buys the fruit with a lock of her golden hair, eats and then sickens, pining ceaselessly for the fruit. Her sister Lizzie courageously visits the goblins, attempts to buy fruit to take back to her dying sister and when refusing to eat with the goblins, endures their vicious attack, which climaxes in her being smeared with the juices of the fruits. But Lizzie is triumphant and 'laughed in heart to feel the drip / Of juices that syruped all her face'. She returns to Laura, covered in juices, which will restore Lizzie to health, as a 'fiery antidote':

She cried, 'Laura,' up the garden,
'Did you miss me?
Come and kiss me.
Never mind my bruises,
Hug me, kiss me, suck my juices
Squeezed from goblin fruits for you.
Goblin pulp and goblin dew.
Eat me, drink me, love me;
For your sake I have braved the glen
And had to do with goblin merchant men.'

Laura 'kissed and kissed her with a hungry mouth', hovers between life and death and eventually awakes, 'as from a dream' to her 'innocent old ways'. She hugs Lizzie, 'but not twice or thrice', showing she has finally learned the value of moderation. This extraordinary poem can be read in many ways: as a cautionary tale, a gothic morality story, a hymn to the wholesomeness of sisterhood or to the taboo of sibling incest, as a religious allegory or a tale of sexual symbolism and libido.

▶ How far can this poem, 'Goblin Market', be compared with *Paradise Lost* and 'The Eve of St Agnes'? What does it have to say about the nature of desire as appetite?

In Ian McEwan's *Atonement*, the fifteen-year-old 'child' Lola (unlike Lizzie in 'Goblin Market') never returns to a state of pre-lapsarian innocence. Lola is given a chocolate bar to eat by her would-be seducer, rapist and future husband, Paul Marshall. The description of Lola consuming the ironically named 'Amo' chocolate bar is written either by Briony as an eighteen-year-old aspiring short-story writer, or by Briony the 78-year-old novelist, and thus the whole passage is consciously over-sexed and arch. Even the name Lola is an abbreviation of Lolita, the pubescent nymphet who is the eponymous heroine of Vladimir Nabokov's controversial novel:

> Paul Marshall sat back in his armchair, watching her closely over the steeple he made with his hands in front of his face.
>   He crossed and uncrossed his legs. Then he took a deep breath.
> 'Bite it,' he said softly. 'You've got to bite it'.
>   It cracked loudly as it yielded to her unblemished incisors, and there was revealed the white edge of the sugar shell, and the dark chocolate beneath it.

Here is Lola's destiny in one paragraph. She will literally be in his hands: he controls her action, and they will be later married. She is virginal, 'unblemished' but yet powerful. She is able not only to penetrate through the outer sugary coating of the bar, but also to reach the darkness inside. She has, through the symbolically named 'Amo' bar, aroused Marshal's lust, as he 'crossed and uncrossed his legs'. Just as the bar 'cracked loudly' through her actions, the rape to come will have violent and destructive repercussions for those around.

THE LITERATURE OF LOVE

Love as a madness

Shakespeare's Sonnet 129 speaks of lust as a compelling madness:

> Th'expense of spirit in a waste of shame
> Is lust in action, and till action, lust
> Is perjured, murd'rous, bloody, full of blame,
> Savage, extreme, rude, cruel, not to trust;
> Enjoyed no sooner but despised straight,
> Past reason hunted, and no sooner had,
> Past reason hated as a swallowed bait
> On purpose laid to make the taker mad:
> Mad in pursuit and in possession so,
> Had, having, and in quest to have, extreme;
> A bliss in proof, and proved, a very woe,
> Before, a joy proposed, behind, a dream.
>   All this the world well knows yet none knows well
>   To shun the heaven that leads men to this hell.

The final word before the rhyming couplet is 'dream', concluding the lengthy first sentence, a sentence restless with desire, weighted with syntactical qualifications and a stream of negatively emotive adjectives. Enjoyment is instantly scorned. 'Bliss' is in proof, a 'woe'. The prepositions 'before' and 'behind' in line 12 (so crucial in Donne's 'To His Mistress Going to Bed' – see page 33, above) here focus the reader's attention on a moment in time, a turning point which renders an imagined happiness, a 'joy', as insubstantial as a 'dream'. The only images in the poem are those of hunting, and of the poisoned 'bait' (features of revenge tragedy), which lead to madness. The final rhyming couplet, by means of a chiasmus 'well know ... knows well' and simple monosyllables, condenses the paradoxical truth expressed throughout the poem – that the pursuit of lust leads us beyond the boundaries of this earth, both to heaven and to hell.

In Middleton and Rowley's revenge play *The Changeling* (1622), the relationship between lust and madness is foregrounded because half the play is set in an asylum where fools and madmen are incarcerated. Beatrice Joanna, the daughter of the Governor of Alicante, initially experiences a passionate sense of revulsion for his facially disfigured servant, aptly named De Flores. She calls him 'serpent', with all the connotations of Satan in the Garden of Eden. But Beatrice's revulsion masks an overwhelming sexual obsession:

> This ominous, ill-faced fellow more disturbs me
> Than all my other passions.   (II.i.53–54)

> I never see this fellow but I think
> Of some harm towards me: danger's in my mind still,
> I scarce leave trembling of an hour after.   (II.i.89–91)

After Beatrice orders him to murder Alonzo, a suitor, De Flores 'deflowers' her as his reward, arranges the murder of her maid, Diaphanta, and finally murders Beatrice before stabbing himself. In the following passage, Alsemero, Beatrice's cuckolded husband, envisages these doomed lovers enacting their passion to an audience of devils, as he pushes them into the closet just before De Flores stabs her, within that dark space. 'Get you into her, sir' also means sexual penetration:

> ALSEMERO: Get you into her, sir. *Exit De Flores (into closet)*
> I'll be your pander now: rehearse again
> Your scene of lust, that you may be perfect
> When you shall come to act it to the black audience
> Where howls and gnashings shall be music to you.
>
> (V.iii.113–117)

We as audience are blind voyeurs, imagining their intercourse in the darkness of hell. Beatrice's cry 'O,O,O' later is both orgasmic, but also, horrifically, her death throes. The lovers, as in Shakespeare's Sonnet 129, are – and will be – in hell.

Demon lovers

In the literature of love, therefore, passion drives lovers both to heaven and to hell. In Shakespeare's tragedy *Othello* (1604) Othello is framed as a demon lover through the machinations of his lieutenant Iago, who persuades him that his wife, Desdemona, is unfaithful to him. Midway through the play, Othello swears revenge. His rhetoric is inflated, full of hellish images. His first words may suggest that it is a performance for his tutor in diabolism, Iago:

> Look here, Iago,
> All my fond love thus do I blow to heaven;
> 'Tis gone:
> Arise, black vengeance, from thy hollow cell!
> Yield up, O love, thy crown and hearted throne
> To tyrannous hate!   (III.iii.445–450)

Later, maddened with jealousy, Othello smothers Desdemona in bed. Even at the very moment of death, Desdemona shows sacrificial love for her husband by lying (see Part 3, page 86). Here, Desdemona's 'lie' reverses the evil of Iago's verbal poison, in order to restore Othello's moral universe, corrupted by Iago. Emilia completes the task. In a kind of exorcism through stichomythia, Emilia blows to pieces Othello's hellish rhetoric. Despite the 'demon' within Desdemona's name, she is 'the more angel' and 'heavenly true'. At the end, Iago maintains an inscrutable silence: Othello recognises that the 'demi-devil / ensnared his soul and body'. His final words, through the anaphora and chiasmus, act as a microcosm of the play 'kissed, killed, killing, kiss':

I kissed thee ere I killed thee: no way but this
Killing myself, to die upon a kiss.

The Romantics and demon lovers

The Romantic poets, Coleridge and Keats, enjoyed conjuring 'demon lovers' in their poetry.

- Coleridge's poem 'Kubla Khan' (1816) contains the following lines describing the 'deep romantic chasm' in Xanadu:

    A savage place, as holy and enchanted
    As e'er beneath a waning moon was haunted
    By woman wailing for her demon lover.

- His gothic ballad of the supernatural, 'Christabel' tells of the mysterious Geraldine who is a serpent in disguise, a female 'demon lover', a *lamia*.

- Keats' 'La Belle Dame Sans Merci' is a *femme fatale* with 'wild eyes', a woman who brings death to many, a demon lover.

- Keats' 'Lamia' is a serpent who is transformed into a beautiful woman by the god Hermes:

    Her head was serpent, but, ah, bitter-sweet!
    She had a woman's mouth with all its pearls complete;
    And for her eyes – what could such eyes do there
    But weep, and weep, that they were born so fair,
    As Proserpine still weeps for her Sicilian air?
    Her throat was serpent, but the words she spake
    Came, as through bubbling honey, for love's sake …

She falls passionately in love with the studious young Corinthian, Lycius, and he reciprocates her love. All is well until Lycius decides to host a magnificent celebratory feast. His old tutor of Philosophy, Apollonius, penetrates Lamia's disguise. Suddenly she shrieks, her beauty falls away, her true serpentine nature is exposed and she vanishes. Lycius dies from grief.

Victorian demon lovers

Does Heathcliff in *Wuthering Heights* (1847) by Emily Brontë (1818–1848) have demonic qualities? Those around him certainly believe so. The narrator, Nelly Dean, at the very end of the novel, discovers Heathcliff alone in a darkened room, near to death, the fire 'smouldered to ashes'. She is appalled at the sight of his face:

'The light flashed on his features, as I spoke. Oh, Mr Lockwood, I cannot express what a terrible start I got, by the momentary view!

Those deep black eyes! That smile, and ghastly paleness! It appeared to me, not Mr Heathcliff, but a goblin; and in my terror, I let the candle bend towards the wall and it left me in darkness.'

Nelly asks herself whether he is a 'ghoul or a vampire'. But how can the most passionate of romantic anti-heroes possibly be compared to a vampire? The earlier episode where Cathy and Heathcliff proclaim their love for the last time upon earth is crucial to our understanding as to whether Heathcliff is 'demonic'.

▶ Read the extract (Part 3, page 87) beginning 'With straining eagerness …' . What is the relationship between violence and passion here?

As Heathcliff approaches his own self-induced death, vibrating with anticipatory, almost religious ecstasy, 'a strong thrilling', he speaks of moving from 'the threshold of hell' to 'within sight of my heaven – I have my eyes on it – hardly three feet to sever me!' The language is sexually charged. Heathcliff becomes, to the neutral observer (Nelly), a demon, a creature not of this world, precisely because he desires to leave it and takes practical steps to do so. He refuses to engage in the rhythm of daily life by eating food. He constructs himself as 'made worse than the devil!' He detaches himself utterly from society as he seeks to attain his heaven by joining 'the relentless one', Catherine, who 'will not shrink' from his company and who has haunted him, structurally from the first pages of the novel, when in a moment of pure gothic horror, the dead waif Cathy had cried 'shiveringly' at the window to be let in. In his terror, Lockwood, the unimaginative narrator responds thus:

As it spoke, I discerned, obscurely, a child's face looking through the window – terror made me cruel; and, finding it useless to attempt shaking the creature off, I pulled its wrist on to the broken pane, and rubbed to and fro till the blood ran down, and soaked the bedclothes.

Surely Lockwood's behaviour, in its viciousness and obsession with blood and bedclothes (sex) is both vampiric and demonic too. The spectre manifested itself to him, rather than Heathcliff, who 'got on to the bed, and wrenched open the lattice, bursting, as he pulled at it, into an uncontrollable passion of tears.

'Come in! come in!' he sobbed. 'Cathy, do come. Oh do – once more! Oh! My heart's darling hear me this time – Catherine, at last!'

But Heathcliff does triumph, achieving his heart's desire, earthly annihilation. Nelly, as above, discovers him lying on his bed 'with a 'frightful, life-like gaze of exultation'. His 'sharp white teeth sneered too!'

I could not think him dead – but his face and throat were washed with rain; the bed-clothes dripped, and he was perfectly still. The lattice, flapping to and fro, had grazed one hand that rested on the sill – no blood trickled from the broken skin, and when I put my fingers to it, I could doubt no more – he was dead and stark!

Note how boundaries are blurred. It appears to be raining inside. A dead man seems alive at first. He has sustained an injury, but there is no blood. The events here structurally reverse the scene at the beginning. Heathcliff has managed this time to open the window (of death) and this time it is his hand, not Cathy's, that is grazed. The rational narrator is Nelly, not Lockwood, who grasps dead flesh. Thus, those observing the elemental passionate love between Catherine and Heathcliff become participants, not in a love story, but what they interpret as a gothic narrative manned by demons.

▶ Consider your reading of vampirism and the demonic in the literature of love, in the light of the following quotations:

'Perhaps sexual desire is only the frustrated desire to eat human flesh. Woman is certainly the best nourishment.' (Novalis, Romantic critic)

'The myth is loaded with sexual excitement; yet there is no mention of sexuality. It is sex without genitalia, sex without confusion, sex without responsibility, sex without guilt, sex without love – better yet, sex without mention.' (James Twitchell, 20th-century critic)

Love as a sickness

The Romantic poet, William Blake, in his poem 'The Sick Rose' (*Songs of Innocence and Experience*, 1789–1794) speaks of the perversely destructive nature of love. This poem may be interpreted symbolically, and Blake, himself an artist, helps the reader to form conclusions through his engraving of the poem:

> O Rose, thou art sick!
> The invisible worm
> That flies in the night,
> In the howling storm,
>
> Has found out thy bed
> Of crimson joy:
> And his dark secret love
> Does thy life destroy.

Tony Kushner, in the two-part play *Angels in America,* writes too of love as a disease, as the dark angel of death winging its way over America, also bringing sickness and destruction – but this time in the form of the AIDS virus. Here, near the beginning of the first play *Millennium Approaches* (1991), the gay lovers Prior and Louis appear to be discussing the non-appearance of their cat, Little Sheba:

> PRIOR: Cats know when something is wrong.
> LOUIS: Only if you stop feeding them.

PRIOR: They know. That's why Sheba left, because she knew.
LOUIS: Knew what?
(Pause)
(He removes his jacket, rolls up his sleeve, shows Louis a dark-purple spot on the underside of his arm near the shoulder)
See.
LOUIS: That's just a burst blood vessel.
PRIOR: Not according to the best medical authorities.
LOUIS: What?
(Pause)
Tell me.
PRIOR: K.S., baby. Lesion number one. Lookit. The wine-dark kiss of the angel of death.
LOUIS *(very softly, holding Prior's arm)*: Oh, please …
PRIOR: I'm a lesionnaire. The Foreign Lesion. The American Lesion. Lesionnaire's disease.
LOUIS: Stop.
PRIOR: My troubles are lesion.

Kushner employs dramatic irony or **prolepsis** here, apparently humorously, but to devastating effect. Louis, like 'Little Sheba', will abandon his suffering lover by simply walking out into the night. The metaphor 'the wine-dark kiss of the angel of death' aptly brings together both the classical world and their Jewish heritage. 'Wine-dark' is a compound adjective employed by Homer in his epic, *The Odyssey*, to describe the sea. Therefore Kushner's use of 'epic' language ensures that the AIDS tragedy, as depicted in *Angels in America,* is given the resonant power of myth. In addition, there is the reference to the angel of death, who passed over the Israelites in Egypt, marking on their door who was to be saved and who killed. Prior, as his name suggests, is chosen to die. He is the first. The manic punning on lesion / legion suggests the frantic battle to come against the disease.

Transgressive love

Transgressive love is a love which strays beyond accepted moral or social boundaries. The Booker prize-winning novel, *The God of Small Things,* by Arundhati Roy (1997) is not narrated chronologically, but the tragedy unfolds in lyrically poetic scenes, often from the point of view of the seven-year-old twins, Estah and Rahel. Abuse, at the hand of the Orangedrink-Lemondrink man in the cinema, eventually causes Estah to become an elective mute, to 'occupy very little space in the world'. The narrator states that 'the reason for his silence was hidden away, entombed somewhere deep in the soothing folds of the fact of it'. The abuse is not mentioned in the therapeutic confessional of the doctor's clinic, as in

Tender is the Night by Scott Fitzgerald (1934), but is described as it occurs in graphic detail from the point of view of seven-year-old Estah, evicted from the auditorium for singing along to *The Sound of Music*. With hideous irony the last words he sings are:

> How do you hold a moonbeam
> *In your hand?*

The abuser, the Orangedrink-Lemondrink man, is seen by the child as 'an unfriendly jewelled bear' – the veneer of civilisation, the jewels, masking the stuff of nightmares, the terror beneath. Like Nicole in *Tender is the Night*, who has been abused by her father, Estah becomes damaged. He is separated from his twin, Rahel, for twenty-three years, but when they are finally united it is in a relationship which defies the prescribed boundaries of love:

> But what was there to say?
>   Only that there were tears. Only that Quietness and Emptiness fitted together like stacked spoons. Only that they held each other close, long after it was over. Only that what they shared that night was not happiness, but hideous grief.
>   Only that once again they broke the Love Laws. That lay down who should be loved. And how. And how much.

The tragedy *'Tis Pity She's a Whore* by John Ford (1633) also 'breaks the love laws' as it tells of a doomed incestuous relationship between a brother and a sister, in a corrupt and unforgiving world. Giovanni pleads for audience understanding of his transgressive love for his sister Annabella, at the end of the play:

> If ever after-times should hear
> Of our fast-knit affections, though perhaps
> The laws of conscience and of civil use
> May justly blame us, yet when they know
> Our loves, that love will wipe away that rigour
> Which would in other incests be abhorred.   (V.v.68–73)

▶ Compare the two extracts above from *The God of Small Things* and *'Tis Pity She's a Whore*. To what extent do both authors appear to exonerate the lovers?

Unrequited love

The speaker in James Fenton's poem 'Nothing' (1983) puts into words the awful truth about unrequited love, that one can do absolutely nothing about it: 'Nothing I can say will make you love me more.' It is a love which is simply not returned. However, rejection, apparent or real, may be the catalyst for inspired literary creation: Petrarch's sonnets to Laura (see Part 1, page 27), the Elizabethan sonnet sequences, *Astrophil and Stella,* by Sir Philip Sidney (1582) and *Amoretti* by Edmund Spenser (1595), as well as many of Shakespeare's sonnets, are finely crafted examples of what the critic Maurice Evans calls 'the poetry of frustration'.

Sir Philip Sidney (1554–1586) began the vogue for writing sonnet sequences. *Astrophil and Stella* is a linked series of 108 sonnets and 11 songs, which charts the unrequited love of Astrophil, the star lover, for Stella, the star. The only event in the entire sequence is a stolen kiss, snatched whilst she sleeps: 'a sugared kiss / In sport I suck'd'. The poet is enamoured of Stella's beauty, and, posing as a Platonic lover, acknowledges the perfection of that form. Yet he still writhes with unsatisfied desire:

> So while thy beautie drawes the heart to love,
> As fast thy Vertue bends that love so good:
> 'But ah,' Desire still cries, 'give me some food.'   (Sonnet 71)

In the conflict of abstract nouns, 'beautie', 'Vertue' and 'Desire', it is Desire that has both an insistently greedy voice, and the last word. Sidney adapted the Italianate Petrarchan sonnet form, employing the enclosed rhyming of the octave, abbaabba, followed by the sestet, cdcdee, to mirror the frustrations of unrequited love, and his own sense of entrapment, in the repeated rhyme of the octave. From the first sonnet onwards the poet seeks 'fit words to paint the blackest face of woe'. But the couplet, with its plosive 'b's provides the answer:

> Biting my truant pen, beating myself for spite,
> 'Foole,' said my Muse to me, 'looke in thy heart, and write.'

▶ Consider Sidney's sonnet 'With how sad steps, Oh Moon, thou climb'st the skies' (Part 3, page 88). What is the poetic effect of the Petrarchan features such as the busy archer with his arrows, eyes, and the moon? How far do you consider this to be a poem in the courtly love tradition?

Philip Sidney's niece, Lady Mary Wroth (1587–1653), wrote *Pamphilia to Amphilanthus* in 1621 (names roughly translate as the all-loving to the 'lover of two', or the faithless one). For Wroth, the Petrarchan convention of love poetry was to prove problematic. How does she communicate desire? She does not employ the traditional rhetoric of the blazon, nor does she make much of eyes. The originality of her poetry lies instead in the psychological realism of the landscape of unrequited love: the dark night, the forest and the strange labyrinth, and also the extraordinarily earthy / pragmatic treatment of the god Cupid. He is no longer the stern controller of destiny, Amor, as seen in Petrarch (see Part 1, page 28) but, apparently, a crying child in need of comfort and compassion. Song 74 expresses Pamphilia's despair. The image of Cupid as a querulous crying child is thoroughly feminine and encapsulates the paradoxically frustrating nature of love in terms of an insistently crying baby, ever demanding, and ever unsatisfied:

> Love a child is ever crying,
> Please him, and he straight is flying,
> Give him, he the more is craving
> Never satisfied with having …

The feminine rhyme highlights the sense of incompletion and lack of satisfaction. This is sustained throughout the five stanzas. The final stanza may conceal a subliminally vicious desire to gain revenge on baby Cupid by exposing him to the wolves:

> Feathers are as firm in staying
> Wolves no fiercer in their praying.
> As a child then leave him crying
> Nor seek him so given to flying.

▶ Consider the sonnet 'Late in the forest I did Cupid see' (Part 3, page 85). How effective do you consider Wroth's nurturing imagery to be? Do the speaker's maternal instincts complement the final Petrarchan twist / conceit at the end?

Unrequited love in Shakespeare

Unrequited lovers are the mainstay of Shakespeare's plays, both comedies and tragi-comedies. Their plight is voiced, obstacles are faced and overcome, and there is predictably a happy resolution, usually marriage. The plays are dramatic and dynamic, moving usually towards satisfactory solutions and resolutions, despite the confusions and pain of the journey. The unfolding of the plot provides dramatic interest. As Viola states in *Twelfth Night,* recognising that Olivia has mistakenly fallen in love with her male disguise, Cesario: 'O time, thou must untangle this, not I; / It is too hard a knot for me t'untie.'

The tangled knot is seen in the following extract. Orsino is extravagantly in love with Olivia, and has employed Viola, disguised as the male Cesario, as his go-between to convey his love. But Viola herself has fallen in love with Orsino, and attempts to communicate this, in code. She is responding to Orsino's pseudo-medical / scientific claim that the woman's body is not physically capable of enduring strong passion. Viola's reply to Orsino is simple and personal. Her disguise falters at the first ellipsis:

VIOLA: Ay, but I know –
ORSINO: What dost thou know?
VIOLA: Too well what love women to men may owe.
               In faith, they are as true of heart as we.

> VIOLA: My father had a daughter loved a man
> As it might be perhaps, were I a woman,
> I should your lordship.
> ORSINO: And what's her history?
> VIOLA: A blank, my lord. She never told her love,
> But let concealment like a worm i' th' bud
> Feed on her damask cheek. She pined in thought,
> And with a green and yellow melancholy
> She sat like Patience on a monument,
> Smiling at grief. Was not this love indeed?
> We men may say more, swear more, but indeed
> Our shows are more than will: for still we prove
> Much in our vows, but little in our love.   (II.iv.106–122)

Her image of the unrequited lover is touching in its simplicity. She creates an emblem of a stoically silent woman, literally 'putting on a brave face'. After the noisy confusion of Orsino's hyperbolic rhetoric, the stately visual portrayal of suffering is affecting.

▶ Compare this extract with Blake's 'The Sick Rose' (page 43, above). How is suffering in love depicted in each? Which images from Viola's speech does Blake borrow?

Victorian unrequited lovers

Charlotte Brontë is not well known for her poetry, yet the undated poem 'He saw my heart's woe, discovered my soul's anguish', has considerable autobiographical and literary significance. The speaker in the poem is Charlotte herself, deeply in love with the married schoolmaster M. Heger who taught her at the Pensionnat in Brussels in 1842. She expressed her feelings towards him in passionate love letters but he forbade her to write more than twice a year. This letter, translated from the French, vividly portrays the strength of her feelings:

> To forbid me to write to you, to refuse to answer me, would be
> to tear from me my only joy on earth … When day by day I await,
> and when day by day disappointment comes to fling me back
> into overwhelming sorrow, and the sweet delight of seeing your
> handwriting and reading your counsel escapes me as a vision that is
> vain – then fever claims me – I lose appetite and I pine away.
>   (Letter, November 18th 1845)

The extremity of her anguish is also expressed in a highly charged emotional lexis in the following poem, the compound adjectives in the last line of the first stanza mirroring the tension between body and soul that is such an essential feature of the unrequited lover. She does not love with her mind alone: her soul is thirsty and feverish. She desires to violate her own flesh, to self-harm, in order to gain a reaction – but to no avail. He is a false god, crafted from stone, incapable of returning love. The somewhat clumsy hexameters only accentuate the intensity of her feelings.

> He saw my heart's woe, discovered my soul's anguish,
> How in fever, in thirst, in atrophy it pined;
> Knew he could heal, yet looked and let it languish, –
> To its moans spirit-deaf, to its pangs spirit-blind.
>
> ...
> Idolater I kneeled to an idol cut in rock!
> I might have slashed my flesh and drawn my heart's best blood:
> The Granite God had felt no tenderness, no shock;
> My Baal had not seen nor heard nor understood.

The poem is surprisingly modern in its reference to self-harm, yet the ending also assumes in its reader – if indeed it was ever meant to have an audience – a strong religious sympathy. Charlotte Brontë's novel, *Villette*, based on her experiences in Brussels, was published in 1853. Both Lucy Snowe in *Villette* and the eponymous Jane Eyre experience extreme raw emotions. Brontë poured into her novels a similar intensity of feeling, as captured in this rough-hewn, awkward poem – which nevertheless convinces through its emotional truth. This, the poem says, is how it feels to be rejected.

Yeats and Maud Gonne

The Irish poet W.B. Yeats (1865–1939) first fell in love with the beautiful Irish nationalist and revolutionary, Maud Gonne, in 1889. She was to be a source of poetic inspiration throughout his life, but she also caused him great sorrow as his love for her was generally considered to be unrequited, although in 1898 she insisted on a 'spiritual marriage'. This is his recollection of their first meeting, from his memoirs:

> I was twenty-three years old when the troubling of my life began.
> I had never thought to see in a living woman so great beauty. It
> belonged to famous pictures, to poetry, to some legendary past. A
> complexion like the blossom of apples, and yet the face and body
> had the beauty of lineaments which Blake calls the highest beauty
> because it changes least from youth to age, and a stature so great
> that she seemed of divine race.

From this moment onwards, Yeats articulated his love for Maud in 'poor words'. Poems inspired by love of Maud include 'The White Birds':

Would that we were, my beloved, white birds on the foam of the sea!
We tire of the flame of the meteor, before it can fade and flee;
And the flame of the blue star of twilight, hung low on the rim of the
sky,
Has awaked in our hearts, my beloved, a sadness that may not die.

The romantic symbolism of the white birds, foam, sea, meteor, flame, blue star, twilight, sky and hearts is to be found in much of the literature of love. In the 'Song of Wandering Aengus', Yeats employs the image of 'the apple blossom' as a coded reference to Maud:

And someone called me by my name:
It had become a glimmering girl
With apple blossom in her hair
Who called me by my name and ran
And faded through the brightening air.

The final stanza combines Irish mythology, the courtly image of the questing lover and the glorious romantic simplicity of imagined fulfilment. Love will never be defeated by the constraints of time:

Though I am old with wandering
Through hollow lands and hilly lands,
I will find out where she has gone,
And kiss her lips and take her hands;
And walk among long dappled grass,
And pluck till time and times are done
The silver apples of the moon,
The golden apples of the sun.

'He Wishes for the Cloths of Heaven', written at the same time, employs the same symbolism of gold and silver light, but has neither the intimacy of 'White Birds', nor the objective ballad-like quality of 'The Song of Wandering Aengus'. And yet it is at the heart of Yeats' poetry, simply because of that word 'poor':

But I, being poor, have only my dreams;
I have spread my dreams under your feet;
Tread softly because you tread on my dreams.

He makes love to his beloved through his poetry. In the poem 'Words' (1910), Yeats imagines quite simply, how it would be, if his 'darling' had understood how he felt:

That she had done so who can say
What would have shaken from the sieve?
I might have thrown poor words away
And been content to live.

'The Folly of being Comforted' is a more intimately personal reflection on unrequited love, through time. Although Yeats adopts the sonnet form, the critic Helen Vendler has pointed out that there is no internal struggle or dialogue. The poet will never be comforted by the helpful friend's cliché that time is a great healer. The fire of her nobility will burn brighter through the years and always arouse in him a passionate longing. Linear time, which brings grey hair and physical decay, merely inflames his desire. The final two lines –

> O heart! O heart! If she'd but turn her head,
> You'd know the folly of being comforted

– with the conditional 'If', the half rhyme 'head / comforted', the antithesis between head and heart, and the head forever turned away from the poet, freeze in a simple gesture: what it is to love and to be ever unrequited.

The proposal

In the literature of love, a proposal may be a formal declaration of intent made by one lover to another, requiring its own special rhetoric since it is both an invitation and an act of persuasion – 'come live with me and be my love'. Conversely, the proposal may come as an unwelcome surprise and also be full of unintentional humour. The woman may seek to deflate the man's ardour through wit, satire or irony. There may too, be motives at work which have very little to do with romantic passion, therefore in a novel the role of the narrator is crucial in guiding the reader's response.

The question of the audience is interesting. How does the recipient respond to the words of the proposal? There may be a hidden audience, listening at the door. From whose point of view do we witness the proposal and how does this affect the narrative? It is useful to consider what weight is given to the proposal itself in the structure of the text and whether it comes as a turning point in the plot.

In *Emma* (1816) Jane Austen's heroine has busied herself throughout the novel as a matchmaker, attempting to find a suitable husband for her protégé Harriet Smith. Mr Knightley has been Emma's moral guardian, not hesitating to correct and chasten her when necessary, but he proposes to Emma almost at the end of the novel. At this point, Emma invites Mr Knightley to continue to think of her as a friend:

> 'I stopped you ungraciously, just now, Mr Knightley, and I am afraid,
> gave you pain. But if you have any wish to speak openly to me as
> a friend, or to ask my opinion of anything that you may have in
> contemplation – as a friend, indeed, you may command me. I will
> hear whatever you like. I will tell you exactly what I think.'

> 'As a friend!' repeated Mr Knightley. 'Emma, that, I fear, is a word
> – no, I have no wish. Stay, yes, why should I hesitate? I have gone too
> far already for concealment. Emma, I accept your offer, extraordinary
> as it may seem, I accept it, and refer myself to you as a friend. Tell
> me, then have I no chance of ever succeeding?'
>
> He stopped in his earnestness to look the question, and the
> expression of his eyes overpowered her.
>
> 'My dearest Emma,' said he, 'for dearest you will always be,
> whatever the event of this hour's conversation, my dearest, most
> beloved Emma – tell me at once. Say "No" if it is to be said.'
>
> She could really say nothing. 'You are silent,' he cried, with great
> animation; 'absolutely silent! At present I ask no more.'
>
> Emma was almost ready to sink under the agitation of the moment.
> The dread of being awakened from the happiest dream was perhaps
> the most prominent feeling.

Emma adopts a formal tone at the beginning. It is worth asking how Mr Knightley responds to her words. Is his language as controlled? What is significant about her silence? Consider the choice of the word 'sink' which is qualified by 'almost' and 'of the moment'. Emma, who has failed disastrously at matchmaking and who has caused trouble for herself and others by speaking out of turn during the course of the novel, has finally learned self knowledge through silence. She allows the other to make her part of his dream. Therefore speech is unnecessary. The superlative 'happiest dream' is not an exaggeration and it is through silence that the writer is able to convey a sense of overwhelming romantic passion.

A century later, during the First World War, the Nottingham writer D.H. Lawrence completed his novel *The Rainbow*. It was initially published in September 1915, then removed from circulation and by the end of November it was banned for obscenity. The story tells of the lives of three generations of the same Nottinghamshire family, the Brangwens. At the beginning of the novel, farmer Tom Brangwen decides the time is ripe to propose to Lydia, the Polish widow who is the housekeeper at the vicarage and mother of little Anna, by her first husband. Tom makes elaborate preparations, symbolically robing himself in his clean white linen shirt, and trimming his beard:

> He put on all clean clothes, folded his stock carefully and donned his
> best coat. Then, being ready, as grey twilight was falling, he went
> across the orchard to gather the daffodils. The wind was roaring in
> the apple-trees, the yellow flowers swayed violently up and down,
> he heard even the fine whisper of their spears as he stooped to break
> the flattened, brittle stems of their flowers.

The first two sentences are measured and sequential. Note the use of assonance and alliteration. The third sentence is a violent contrast. The wind disturbs and unsettles. Brangwen's relationship with the natural world is as intimate as a man with his lover. He is attuned to the whisper of the leaves. The powerful wind surrounds him. He 'stoops to break' the flowers. Why should a proposal take place on a stormy spring night? The novel's title, *The Rainbow*, is relevant. In the Biblical account of the Flood, the rainbow was sent by God after the Flood as a sign of hope and of new beginnings, as a covenant or 'engagement' between God and his people. A proposal marks the beginning of a new life.

Later in the novel, Lydia's daughter, Anna, now eighteen, participates in a moonlit harvest with her cousin Will. The gathering in of the corn sheaves becomes the dance of courtship, described with lyrical physicality: 'They stooped, grasped the wet, strong hair of the corn, lifted the heavy bundles, and returned.' Lawrence, through his narration, builds insistently towards an orgasmic climax, seemingly forever deferred:

> Why was there always a space between them, why were they apart? Why, as she came up from under the moon, would she halt and stand off from him? Why was he held away from her? His will drummed persistently, darkly, it drowned everything else.

Lawrence uses the metaphor of 'drowning', as Jane Austen used 'sink' earlier, to describe an overwhelming, passionate force. Is Lawrence punning on Will's name, referring to physical arousal? *The Rite of Spring,* a ballet choreographed by Diaghilev, with music by the composer Stravinsky, depicts a pagan ritual of a young girl dancing herself to death. This too was written in the early 20th century, between 1912 and 1913, and it too caused uproar at the first performance, owing to its insistently rhythmical sexual content. The relentless percussive rhythm is of a piece with Lawrence's writing: 'His will drummed darkly, persistently… Into the rhythm of his work there came pulse and steadied purpose.' Finally, the lovers come together, transfigured by the moonlight, and charged with the rhythm of their movement. Will proposes to Anna (see Part 3, page 88).

▶ Why do you think that Lawrence so insistently uses repetition, in his language and his sentence structure? What part do landscape and the night-time play?

In a much more light-hearted vein than Lawrence, Oscar Wilde (1854–1900) has the two young women in *The Importance of Being Earnest* (1895), Cecily and Gwendolen, clearly stage manage their own proposals. Gwendolen has outlined her game plan: 'My ideal has always been to love someone of the name of Ernest.' Therefore her plan must be put into operation and the formalities of proposals must be observed. Jack, whom Gwendolen believes to be called Ernest, must follow her script (see Part 3, page 90).

The Importance of Being Earnest is a comedy of manners. Gwendolen's tone is forthright and commanding, demonstrated by her use of short, clipped sentences. She assumes the male role. Jack's responses are conditioned by her unnerving formality. Meanwhile, Gwendolen's mother, the imperious Lady Bracknell, sails in. But Gwendolen must ensure that the proposal is complete. She verbally suppresses her mother and physically keeps her fiancé at her feet:

> Mamma! (*He tries to rise; she restrains him*) I must beg you to retire. This is no place for you. Besides, Mr Worthing has not finished yet.

It is, ironically, the Gorgon Lady Bracknell who makes the surprisingly romantic point that 'An engagement should come upon a young girl as a surprise, pleasant or unpleasant as the case may be.'

Another extraordinary 'virtual' proposal occurs in the modernist novel *Vile Bodies* (1930) by Evelyn Waugh (1903–1966). Adam, as Everyman, is the novel's supposed hero. Nina is his lover (see Part 3, page 90). Experimentally, Evelyn Waugh uses the telephone here as a narrative device. The repeated phrase 'I see' therefore becomes increasingly ironic as the conversation develops. The lovers are physically separated, holding two separate telephones, and yet Waugh does not make it easy for the reader to identify who is speaking. There is considerable repetition and syntactic parallelism as the speakers appear to blur identity. The flat, laconic and monosyllabic speech, which appears to be a world away from Oscar Wilde's polished dialogue, feeds the emptiness. Chapter 11 is a microcosm of the whole text. Adam and Nina's relationship has crumbled and disintegrated. Later in the novel, Nina marries Ginger, leaving Adam alone. The tone of the novel darkens considerably. By the end of the novel, society has tumbled into war and the days of the bright young things are over. The final sentence of the novel reads: 'And presently, like a circling typhoon, the sounds of battle began to return.'

The wedding

Weddings are represented in the literature of love as both endings and beginnings. As proposals are often theatrical, involving some dialogue between the couple, it is more usual to find proposals in novels or plays, as we have seen. However, the symbolic liturgy of the wedding lends itself to poetry. Like poetry, weddings encapsulate or condense a moment in time. Indeed, a carefully chosen poem is often read during the wedding ceremony.

It may therefore be useful to begin the study of the ceremony of weddings in literature by examining a poem and an extract from a novel, both often heard at weddings. Shakespeare's Sonnet 116 echoes language from the Marriage Service in the Book of Common Prayer: 'if either of you know any impediment [obstacle], why ye may not be lawfully joined together in Matrimony, ye do now confess it.'

Let me not to the marriage of true minds
Admit impediments; love is not love
Which alters when it alteration finds,
Or bends with the remover to remove.
O, no, it is an ever fixed mark
That looks on tempests and is never shaken;
It is the star to every wandering bark,
Whose worth's unknown, although his height be taken.
Love's not Time's fool, though rosy lips and cheeks
Within his bending sickle's compass come;
Love alters not with his brief hours and weeks,
But bears it out even to the edge of doom.
    If this be error and upon me proved,
    I never writ, nor no man ever loved.

The second passage is from *Captain Corelli's Mandolin* (1994) by Louis de
Bernières. The story is set during the Second World War on the Greek island of
Cephalonia. The local doctor's daughter has fallen in love with Captain Corelli,
a member of the occupying Italian force. Here, her father talks to her about the
nature of love:

> Love is a temporary madness, it erupts like volcanoes and then
> subsides. And when it subsides you have to make a decision. You
> have to work out whether your roots have so entwined together that
> it is inconceivable that you should ever part. Because this is what
> love is. Love is not breathlessness, it is not excitement, it is not the
> promulgation of promises of eternal passion … Love itself is what
> is left over when being in love has burned away, and this is both an
> art and a fortunate accident. Your mother and I had it, we had roots
> that grew towards each other underground, and when all the pretty
> blossoms had fallen from our branches we found that we were one
> tree and not two.

The speaker in Shakespeare's sonnet appears to rise as a member of the
congregation at a marriage service at the very point when the question is intoned.
It is questionable whether, logically, 'love is not love / Which alters as it alteration
finds' follows from the commanding opening 'Let me not to the marriage of true
minds / Admit impediments'. In the wedding service the exhortation to reveal any
'impediments' occurs *before* the marriage is solemnised. Shakespeare however,
decrees that the love to come will transcend the 'impediments' of time and space.
The marriage in this poem is one of 'true minds', although in the Marriage Service
the man only says: 'With my body I thee worship.' There is a sense of linguistic
marriage or pairing in the poem – words are gently coupled or wedded together:
'love … love', 'alters … alteration', 'remover … remove'. The speaker next provides

a solemn discourse on the enduring and eternal nature of love and appears to be actually assuming the role of the priest. Over half of the poem, syntactically, is controlled by the word 'not', which – although apparently defying the ravages of time – raises questions through its very negativity.

Dr Iannis, in *Captain Corelli's Mandolin,* also appears to be tenderly preaching to his daughter. The explosive nature of erotic passion is dismissed as a madness, as an 'erupting volcano'. Rationality takes over: '… you have to make a decision. You have to work out …'. Like Shakespeare, Louis de Bernières uses the word 'not' to powerful effect. He distinguishes between 'love' and 'being in love'. Love is the residue after the 'being in love' stage has burned itself away. The imagery of fires and volcanoes is replaced with the natural metaphor of the roots uniting underground, so that in time, when the 'pretty blossoms' have fallen, the couple discover that they are one. Time may destroy 'rosy lips and cheeks' and cause petals to fall, but paradoxically, it is through time that love is revealed. Both writers use imagery of place to emphasise the relationship between time and the eternal: Shakespeare reaches for the skies, providing a visual and auditory (assonance) navigational triangle in the text made by the words 'star, mark, bark', whereas de Bernières delves underground, celebrating the union in earthly terms.

In the literature of love, an *epithalamion* (from the Greek meaning 'at the bedroom door') is a poem celebrating a marriage, traditionally sung at the door of the bridal chamber on the wedding night. It has its origins in classical literature, and was revived in the Renaissance. Blessings and prayers for a fertile and happy marriage are heaped upon the couple. The poet pays tribute to the beauty of the bride, as well as giving an account of the wedding day, a kind of literary wedding video.

Probably the most famous *epithalamion* is that written by Edmund Spenser in 1594, as a wedding present for his bride, Elizabeth Boyle. The wedding took place in Ireland, and he blends references to classical deities, the Christian church calendar and the Irish landscape in a mathematically satisfying *tour de force*. The poem has 365 long lines, one for every day of the year, and twenty-four stanzas, one for every hour of the day. The actual wedding of the couple, the church ceremony, forms the central part of the poem. The poem is full of the features of conventional love poetry; birds perform a special concert of their own:

> Hark how the cheerful birds do chant their lays
> And carols of love's praise.

The learned sisters, the Muses, inspire the poet at the outset to 'resound love's praises'. The nymphs of Mulla, an Irish river, are instructed to make the waters, teeming with trout and pike, as clear as crystal for the bride.

▶ Consider the extract from Spenser's 'Epithalamion' (Part 3, page 80). How does Spenser describe the emergence of the bride? What is the effect of the blazon? Compare this with the passage from the *Song of Songs* (Part 1, page 14). What similarities do you notice? How sensuous is the language?

Shakespeare concludes *A Midsummer Night's Dream* with an *epithamalion*. The king of the fairies, Oberon, arrives with his fairy retinue, to 'bless this place':

> OBERON: Now, until the break of day,
> Through this house each fairy stray.
> To the best bride-bed will we,
> Which by us shall blessed be;
> And the issue there create
> Ever shall be fortunate.   (V.i.379–384)

A wedding here is an occasion of unification, where two become one, symbolised by the joining of hands. Earth and heaven (or fairyland) rejoice. Threats of disharmony and disunity are banished.

The marriage which disturbs

In the literature of love, the marriage ceremony, or an account of the marriage, can sometimes unsettle the reader. Chaucer, in *The Merchant's Tale,* describes the wedding between the aged Januarie and young 'fresshe' May thus:

> But finally ycomen is the day
> That to the chirche bothe be they went
> For to receyve the hooly sacrement.
> Forth comth the preest, with stole aboute his nekke.
> And bad hire be lyk Sarra and Rebekke   (*hire* her)
> In wisdom and in trouthe of mariage,
> And seyde his orisons, as is usage,   (*orisons* prayers)
> And croucheth hem, and bad God sholde hem blesse,
> And made al siker ynogh with hoolinesse.   (*siker* binding)

At first glance, everything seems in order. The day arrives, the couple go to church, the priest blesses them and binds them together with holiness. However, the wedding is both tedious and hasty. The priest appears to be going through the motions, as suggested by the cynical tone of 'made al siker ynogh with hoolinesse' and of 'as is usage'. Rebecca is an alarming role model for a bride. She was a successfully cunning and deceitful figure in the Old Testament. This reference signposts May's later deception of Januarie and even her cuckolding of him, as she frolics up the pear tree with the young squire Damyon.

By contrast with Chaucer's cold satire, a disturbingly vicious account of a marriage is related in the play *Who's Afraid of Virginia Woolf?* (1962) by Edward Albee. The action of the play takes place very late one evening on an American campus university after a party, when George and Martha are joined by a younger couple, Nick and Honey, for further drinks. Some see it as the unbinding, or disintegration of two marriages. Certainly lies, deceits, phantom pregnancies and birthing ghost children are all part of the drama. Drunken disclosures of hidden secrets surface. In Act 2, *Walpurgisnacht* (exorcism), the host, George, decides that the four of them are in the process of playing a series of cruelly alliterative games: ' Humiliate the Host' …, 'Hump the Hostess'. The next is to be 'Get the Guests'. In an extract from this game (Part 3, page 91), George relates the circumstances of the marriage of Mouse and Blondie as though he is telling a 'what happened next' fairy story to children. Thinly disguised, the Mouse is Honey and Blondie is Nick. George's game provokes extreme reactions. Honey rushes off to vomit. Nick is exposed and humiliated as he has previously provided George with the ammunition for this attack. Honey had tricked Nick into marriage through a phantom pregnancy, a 'pouf'. The onomatopoeic 'pouf' neatly expresses George's controlled rage. The stage directions too are subtly effective and ironic. George speaks 'as if to a baby', which there never was. It is the male partner who is 'nearly sick'. Honey 'grabs at her belly' although she is not pregnant. The motives for their wedding were as insubstantial and ephemeral as a fairy story. The 'Mouse' in George's tale within the play is one dimensional, a female Mickey Mouse, the archetypal and iconic American cartoon figure.

▶ Read the passage on page 91. What does this passage say about the nature of American marriage and society as Albee portrays them?

The honeymoon

Probably one of the most joyful honeymoons in the literature of love is that taken by the middle generation of the Brangwen family, Will and Anna, in *The Rainbow*. Lawrence suspends his lovers away from time and space, in their own newly created world of love. Above all else, his language is religious: 'And to him, it was as if the heavens had fallen, and he were sitting with her among the ruins, in a new world …'. Lawrence describes Will's astonishment at his rebirth into the new world of married love thus:

> One day, he was a bachelor, living with the world. The next day, he was with her, as remote from the world as if the two of them were buried like a seed in darkness. Suddenly, like a chestnut falling out of a burr, he was shed naked and glistening on to a soft, fecund earth, leaving behind him the hard rind of worldly experience and knowledge.

> It was all very well at night, when the doors were locked and the darkness drawn around them. Then they *were* the only inhabitants of the visible earth, and the rest were under the flood. And being alone in the world, they were a law unto themselves, they could enjoy and squander and waste like conscienceless gods.

▶ Consider the effect of the chestnut simile. What does it suggest about male and female sexuality? How does Lawrence create a sense of new beginnings?

The word 'honeymoon' suggests sensual pleasures taken at night, but also hints that all pleasure is fleeting and temporary, that passion waxes and wanes like the moon.

In Victorian times, the honeymoon often involved a journey taken by the newlyweds to a place of cultural, historic and romantic interest. Venice, Verona and Rome were popular destinations. In the novel *Middlemarch* (1871–1872) by George Eliot, the heroine, Dorothea and her elderly, clerical husband Mr Casaubon indeed honeymoon in Rome, where Mr Casaubon spends all day in the Vatican library researching 'the key to all mythologies', while Dorothea, idealistic, ardent and romantic, visits galleries and ancient ruins. But Dorothea is neglected by her husband, and she begins to view his *magnum opus*, his great work, *The Key to All Mythologies*, as trite, petty and pointless. George Eliot begins Chapter 20 of *Middlemarch* with the image of Dorothea, seated in her boudoir, sobbing bitterly. She is disillusioned and alone:

> How was it that in the weeks since her marriage, Dorothea had not distinctly observed but felt with a stifling depression, that the large vistas and wide fresh air which she had dreamed of finding in her husband's mind were replaced by ante-rooms and winding passages which seemed to lead nowhither? I suppose it was in courtship everything is regarded as provisional and preliminary, and the smallest sample of virtue or accomplishment is taken to guarantee delightful stores which the broad leisure of marriage will reveal. But the door-sill of marriage once crossed, expectation is concentrated on the present. Having once embarked on your marital voyage, it is impossible not to be aware that you make no way and that the sea is not in sight – that, in fact, you are exploring an enclosed basin.

▶ How does George Eliot create a sense of entrapment within marriage here? Consider the imagery used. How does the authorial voice add weight to the passage? What is the relationship between the metaphorical and the literal?

George Eliot herself honeymooned in both Verona and Venice, but on the 16th June 1880 a calamity occurred. Her husband, John Cross, jumped from his hotel window into the Grand Canal below. He survived but his motives remained a mystery. He may have been suffering from depression, or he may have felt overwhelmed by the intellectual powers of his considerably older wife. It is not known whether the marriage had been consummated at that stage. The biographer Walter Sichel wrote cynically in 1923: 'It was rumoured that after a prolonged course of Dante at Venice he had cast himself into the Grand Canal and begged the gondoliers not to rescue him.'

Writing in Chapter One, 'Reading Honeymoons' of *Victorian Honeymoons: Journeys to the Conjugal* (2006), Helena Michie identifies several disastrous literary honeymoons. These are some of them:

> In the realm of fiction, perhaps the place to begin is the shortest honeymoon: Victor Frankenstein's abortive trip to Evian, where his bride Elizabeth Lavenza, is murdered and probably raped by the monster as Victor ponders the Alpine Scenery that was to become so central to Victorian ideals of the wedding journey. …
> The honeymoons in *Tess of the D'Urbervilles* and *Daniel Deronda* share elements of the honeymoon gothic: apparitions, spectral or otherwise, of other women and illegitimate sexual pasts; haunted jewels and symbolic caskets that in *Tess* are literal coffins, sleepwalking and female hysteria.

The most catastrophic honeymoon in recent literary times has to be the honeymoon in the novella *On Chesil Beach* by Ian McEwan (2007). Here, the couple are not separated by age (unlike Januarie and May in *The Merchant's Tale*) or by sexual experience. Both are twenty-two and virgins. The events in the novel take place in 1962, a significant date, as it precedes the *Lady Chatterley's Lover* trial by a year:

> Sexual intercourse began in 1963
> (Though just too late for me)
> Between the end of the Chatterley ban
> And the Beatles' first LP.   (Philip Larkin)

Edward and Florence are to spend the first night of their honeymoon in a hotel on Chesil Beach in Dorset. McEwan explores the relationship between romantic love and the mechanics of sexual love. Both Edward and Florence appear to love each other romantically, but both are virgins and have a patchy understanding of the workings of the bodies of the opposite sex. The 1960s honeymoon meal and then the attempts to consummate the marriage are described in clinical detail. Here it is hard to escape the uncomfortable feeling that the reader has become a voyeur, a watcher at the door. Like Januarie, Florence has read up on technique, or what happens in sexual intercourse from 'a modern, forward looking guide':

> In optimistic moments she tried to convince herself that she suffered
> no more than a heightened form of squeamishness which was bound
> to pass … and the idea of herself being touched 'down there' by
> someone else, even someone she loved, was as repulsive as, say, a
> surgical procedure on her eye.

The phrase 'someone else, even someone she loved' appears innocuous but the author hints earlier in the novel that Florence may have been abused by her father. McEwan had stated in a pre-2008 Booker prize interview:

> In the final draft it's there as a shadowy fact for readers to make of it
> what they will. I didn't want to be too deterministic about this. Many
> readers may miss it altogether, which is fine.

Therefore to cope, or even to survive and maintain her sanity, Florence detaches her mind from the invasion, regarding it forensically as an 'operation'. There is an irony in the simile 'a surgical procedure on her eye': in the Petrarchan / courtly love tradition, love enters through the eye. Edward has no chance. Florence rushes out onto Chesil Beach, where the couple accuse each other of being 'frigid' and 'disgusting' respectively. Tragically, like the final stanza of Matthew Arnold's love poem, 'Dover Beach' (1867) which reverberates throughout the novel, the lovers do not remain 'true to one another', but instead the final three lines of the poem are applicable:

> And we are here as on a darkling plain
> Swept with confused alarms of struggle and flight,
> Where ignorant armies clash by night.

They separate, never to see each other again. The unconsummated marriage is annulled. But their lives have been altered forever. McEwan writes: 'That is how the entire course of a life can be changed – by doing nothing.'

Are honeymoons ever comic? We have seen Dorothea's distress, the calamitous failure in *On Chesil Beach,* and the vital passion of Will and Anna. Edward Lear's poem *The Owl and the Pussy-Cat* (1871) charmingly includes courtship, marriage and honeymoon within its three whimsical verses. Here, two disparate creatures embark on a sea journey together, providentially packing items which will provide for their economic security and physical well-being (money and honey). Indeed, the honey is an emblem, which anticipates the celebratory honeymoon in the last stanza. Gender is indeterminate. It is commonly assumed that the Owl is male, Pussy female, but it is not stated. The Owl seeks inspiration from the stars for his 'charmingly sweet' love ditty. Pussy is anxious. It is time to wed, but they need a ring. All is resolved in the approved fairytale manner. The poem ends in a dance, in true Shakespearean fashion.

Surprisingly, this poem, with its declaration of love, a romantic journey, a wedding, a wedding feast and a moonlight beach dance, is the quintessence of romance. It celebrates and rejoices in difference. The most unlikely creatures may happily wed. The extraordinary oddness of the world in which we live is not to be feared, but utilised and embraced, and as a result, love views the world as beautiful, semantically unified. This is made clear from the outset:

> The Owl and the Pussy-Cat went to sea
> In a beautiful pea-green boat
> They took some honey and plenty of money
> Wrapped up in a five-pound note.
> The Owl looked up to the stars above
> And sang to a small guitar,
> 'O lovely Pussy! O Pussy, my love,
> What a beautiful pussy you are,
> You are,
> You are!
> What a beautiful pussy you are!'

Married love

The poet Coventry Patmore (1823–1896) certainly believed in the importance of romantic love within marriage. His epic poem *The Angel in the House* (1854–1863), extols both the physical and spiritual joys of married love, and draws upon Aristophanes' account of the separated beings in the *Symposium* (see Part 1, page 9). This concept of the 'angel in the house' became part of the **zeitgeist** of the latter part of the 19th century, epitomising everything that Queen Victoria held precious, so much so that it was sometimes cynically referred to as the 'Albert in the house'. But, writing in the 20th century, Virginia Woolf, in her lecture on 'Professions for Women' (1931), urged women writers to 'kill the Angel in the house'. No more suppliant, passive middle class domesticity. No more doe-eyed little Victorian women, such as Charles Dickens' sugary character Dora, the child-bride, happily worshipping the patriarchal authority of her husband, David Copperfield.

And what of the woman's voice? Elizabeth Barrett Browning (1806–1861) secretly married the poet Robert Browning in 1846, after a passionate exchange of love letters. The development of her love for Browning is to be seen in the sonnet sequence *Sonnets from the Portuguese* (published 1850). Deliberately chosen to mislead the reader into assuming that the sonnet sequence was a translation, 'Portuguese' was in fact Browning's affectionate nickname for Elizabeth. Always aware, as she is, of her own invalid status, her love for Browning blossoms into reciprocal joy. The most famous sonnet occurs late in the sequence: 'How do I love thee? Let me count the ways' (XLII). At this stage she is assured of Browning's love and the sonnet mirrors her serene confidence. Sonnet XXIII expresses in dramatic terms her realisation of Browning's love for her.

▶ Consider the theatrical qualities of this sonnet (Part 3, page 92). What is the relationship between love and religious faith?

Happily ever after?

In the novels of Jane Austen, marriage is the condition to which all aspire: it provides economic security, a respectable position in society and the possibility of lasting happiness. But errors of judgement are made and exposed along the way, whether through faulty self-knowledge or a readiness to be dazzled by the superficial and worldly charms of those without true principles. Emma has to learn humility. Elizabeth Bennett must divest herself of her prejudices. Marianne, 'sensible' to the flirtatious advances of the desirable but unprincipled Willoughby, eventually learns to value the sterling goodness of the family friend, Colonel Brandon. Catherine Morland, in *Northanger Abbey*, learns not to read the world as a gothic novel, with herself as the eagerly tremulous victim, but to function in society as a rational adult.

On the other hand, the heroines of *Persuasion, Mansfield Park*, and to a lesser extent *Sense and Sensibility* endure many afflictions with stoical fortitude and courage, before their true worth is recognised. Anne Eliot in *Persuasion*, whose 'bloom has faded', must witness Captain Wentworth, the man she loves dearly, become drawn to the younger and more sparky, frivolous and skittish Musgrove sisters. Elinor, in *Sense and Sensibility*, falls in love with Edward Ferrars, only to discover that he has been engaged to another woman for four years. Fanny Price, bullied by her Aunt Norris in *Mansfield Park,* and treated indifferently by her lively cousins, has to watch the man she loves, her cousin Edmund, mesmerised by the dangerously worldly charms of Mary Crawford. Moreover, Fanny is party, on an almost daily basis, to his romantic confidences. But all ends well. In each novel, virtue finds its own reward: marriage.

All these marriages occur at the end of the novels. But what of those who marry during the course of the novel? In *Pride and Prejudice* (1813) Elizabeth Bennett has firmly rejected the unctuous clergyman Mr Collins, but is startled to discover that her dear friend Charlotte Lucas has accepted him. Jane Austen reveals Charlotte's reasoning:

> Charlotte herself was tolerably composed. She had gained her
> point and had time to consider of it. Her reflections were in general
> satisfactory. Mr Collins to be sure was neither sensible nor agreeable;
> his society was irksome, and his attachment to her must be
> imaginary. But he would still be her husband. Without thinking highly
> of either men or of matrimony, marriage had always been her object;
> it was the only honourable provision for well-educated young ladies
> of small fortune, and however uncertain of giving happiness, must be

their pleasantest preservative from want. This preservative she had now obtained; and at the age of twenty-seven, without having ever been handsome, she felt all the good luck of it.

The success or otherwise of the marriage is seen from Elizabeth's perspective, as she is invited to stay for an extended period at the vicarage, the nuptial home of the newly wed Reverend and Mrs Collins. At the beginning of her stay, in the 'solitude of her chamber', Elizabeth 'had to meditate upon Charlotte's degree of contentment, to understand her address in guiding, and composure in bearing with, her husband and to acknowledge that it was all done very well.' Elizabeth's emotions are more evident later, on departure, as she empathises with Charlotte's lot:

> Poor Charlotte! – it was melancholy to leave her to such society! – But she had chosen it with her eyes open; and though evidently regretting that her visitors were to go, she did not seem to ask for compassion. Her home and her housekeeping, her parish and her poultry, and all their dependent concerns, had not yet lost their charms.

The impersonal pronoun 'it' in the second sentence may refer to the state of marriage or, more cruelly, Mr Collins. The wittily ironic alliterative linking of 'parish and poultry' implies that hens loom as large as parishioners. 'Yet' is a disquieting word, hinting that in time, domestic bliss will pall. The novel, however, is Elizabeth Bennett's story and therefore this may simply be read as a further example of Elizabeth's prejudice.

▶ What, according to Austen, is the relationship between rationality and emotion?

Shades of the prison house

The reader understands that Charlotte has married Mr Collins as a kind of life insurance policy. Romantic happiness is an irrelevance. Isabel Archer, the heroine in Henry James' (1843–1916) novel *The Portrait of a Lady* (1881), also marries midway through the story, but, unlike Charlotte, she is free to choose from a wide variety of suitable suitors. She is a beautiful, idealistic and spirited American, who receives offers of marriage from several eligible men, both European and American. The collector of fine art treasures, Gilbert Osmond, wins her love and trust, and she marries him. But she is no more to him than a fine art treasure, a portrait, and a rich source of wealth to be exploited.

▶ Consider the passage from *The Portrait of a Lady* (Part 3, page 93). At this point in the novel, Isabel has been married for over a year. What is the effect of the imagery? How does James convey her state of mind?

The image of married life as 'a dark narrow alley with a dead wall at the end', as seen in the Henry James passage, is brutal in its finality. Vicki Feaver, in her poem 'The Crack' (Part 3, page 93), similarly employs an image from masonry, an extended metaphor or conceit of a crack materialising in a home, to suggest that a relationship has rocky foundations and that the couple are unwittingly becoming estranged. It also highlights in concrete terms the couple's willingness to collude with each other in ignoring the fissure in their relationship until it is too late.

Momentous questions about the nature of married love are asked by Janie in *Their Eyes Were Watching God* (1937) by the African-American writer Zora Neale Hurston (1891–1960):

> There are years that ask questions and years that answer. Janie had had no chance to know things so she had to ask. Did marriage end the cosmic loneliness of the unmated? Did marriage compel love like the sun the day?

She marries twice, both times unhappily, before she falls joyfully in love with the irresistible and feckless Tea Cake. The extract in Part 3 (page 94) marks the point in the novel where Janie realises the true state of her marriage to her second husband, Jody. The adjective 'marital' shifts its letters to become 'martial'. Violence supersedes love.

▶ The extract is an **epiphany**. What has Janie realised about her marriage? Consider the link between concrete domestic detail and internal soulfulness. Why do you think the writer chose to tell Janie's story in the third person?

Isabel Archer in *The Portrait of a Lady* is imprisoned within her marriage in the 'realms of restriction and depression where the sound of other lives, freer and easier, was heard as from above, and where it served to deepen the feeling of failure'. Likewise, Janie's marital unhappiness is described later as 'a rut in the road. Plenty of life beneath the surface but it was kept beaten down by the wheels.' Both writers blend an emotional state – depression and unhappiness – with the metaphor of being downtrodden, of being incarcerated in an earthly hell. Indeed, James' writing here owes something to Milton's description of Hell, a landscape of psychological torment, in the first book of his epic *Paradise Lost*.

Also writing about entrapment, the novelist and poet George Meredith (1828–1909) charts the hellish disintegration of a marriage in the thinly veiled autobiographical narrative sonnet sequence *Modern Love* (1862). The sonnets, unusually, have sixteen lines:

> At dinner, she is hostess, I am host,
> Went the feast ever cheerfuller? She keeps
> The Topic over intellectual deeps

In buoyancy afloat. They see no ghost.
With sparkling surface-eyes we ply the ball;
It is in truth a most contagious game:
HIDING THE SKELETON shall be its name.
Such play as this the devils might appal!
But here's the great wonder; in that we,
Enamoured of an acting nought can tire,
Each other, like true hypocrites, admire;
Warm-lighted looks, Love's Ephemerae,　　　(*Ephemerae* short-lived
Shoot gaily o'er the dishes and the wine.　　　　　　　creatures)
We waken envy of our happy lot.
Fast, sweet and golden, shows the marriage-knot.
Dear guests, you have now seen Love's corpse-light shine.

(Sonnet XVII)

The couple maintain the hypocrisy of a respectable Victorian middle-class couple
hosting a dinner party. The Petrarchan conceit of the arrows of love fired into the
heart of the beloved is used to provide a hypocritical cover, an illusion of marital
happiness. There is a gothic interplay between light and death, which climaxes in
the oxymoronic 'corpse-light'. This was, traditionally, a flame seen in a graveyard
and interpreted as an omen of death. The personified death of Love, of their
marriage, is revealed with a dramatic flourish at the end of the sonnet, much as a
conjuror may amaze his audience with the unexpected. Is it all a game, in which
the estranged couple take vicious pleasure, and which, ironically, unites them both
as performers, with a grim secret, and in masochistic pain?

▶ Compare the sonnet above with the extract from *Who's Afraid of Virginia Woolf?*
(Part 3, page 91). To what extent do Meredith and Albee appear to see entrapment
as a game played by a married couple for the benefit of an audience?

What will survive of us is love

But love in marriage can and does survive. In *Who's Afraid of Virginia Woolf?*
Martha, in Act 3: The Exorcism, astonishes Nick by informing him that George, her
husband, is the only man in her life who has ever made her happy:

> MARTHA: George who is out there somewhere in the dark … George
> who is good to me, and whom I revile; who understands me, and
> whom I push off; who can make me laugh, and I choke it back in
> my throat; who can hold me, at night, so that it's warm, and whom
> I will bite so there's blood; who keeps learning the games we play
> as quickly as I can change the rules; who can make me happy and I
> do not wish to be happy, and yes I do wish to be happy. George and
> Martha: sad, sad, sad.

Martha and George, like the couple in *Modern Love,* have been playing games. But here the woman speaks to an incredulous and disbelieving outsider of her love for George, her husband, a marital love which embraces disharmony, rejection, vampire-like violence and emotional irrationality and instability. The following measured cadences read like a religious litany of love:

> who tolerates, which is intolerable; who is kind, which is cruel; who understands, which is beyond comprehension ...

The repeated oxymorons have their roots in the tradition of courtly love (see Part 1, page 22).

Marital love may transcend death. Janie, in *Their Eyes Were Watching God* by Zora Neale Hurston, has married her third husband, Tea Cake. The sensuous lyricism of the writing, which describes her love for him, echoes the *Song of Songs*:

> He looked like the love thoughts of women. He could be a bee to a blossom – a pear tree blossom in the spring. He seemed to be crushing scent out of the world with his footsteps. Crushing aromatic herbs with every step he took. Spices hung about him. He was a glance from God.

But tragedy strikes. In rescuing Janie from the flood which brings death to the coasts of the Southern States of America, Tea Cake is bitten on the cheek by a rabid dog. In self-defence, Janie shoots her deranged husband, who in his delirium has been intent on murdering her. She is exonerated at her trial. Afterwards Janie reflects on her love for Tea Cake:

> Dis house ain't so absent of things lak it used tuh be befo' Tea Cake come along. It's full uh thoughts, 'specially dat bedroom ...
>   Love is lak de sea. It's uh movin' thing, but still and all, it takes its shape from de shore it meets, and it's different with every shore ...

> Then Tea Cake came prancing around here where she was and the song of the sigh flew out of the window and lit in the top of the pine trees. Tea Cake, with the sun for a shawl. Of course he wasn't dead. He could never be dead until she herself had finished feeling and thinking. The kiss of his memory made pictures of love and light against the wall. Here was peace. She pulled in her horizon like a great fish-net. Pulled it from around the waist of the world and draped it over her shoulder. So much of life in its meshes! She called in her soul to come and see ...

▶ Consider the use of African/American colloquial speech in this passage. How original do you find the simile of the sea?

▶ How effective do you find the last paragraph as the ending to the novel? Compare it with the final paragraphs of any love stories you have read.

Love and loss

Throughout literature, there have been lovers who have become famous through the intensity of their love, and the tragic nature of its end. The apparent timelessness of the lover's passion is destroyed by death, yet it is through literature that the mortal love of doomed lovers is immortalised. Shakespeare's Romeo and Juliet and Antony and Cleopatra are the archetypal doomed lovers: Romeo and Juliet, dying as scarcely more than children, within the enclosed world of Verona, having loved each other for a few short days; Antony and Cleopatra, mighty rulers and conquerors of the known ancient world, having been lovers for many years.

Both Antony and Cleopatra consciously immortalise their love and project their own deaths as a theatrical spectacle. Antony imagines a pastoral heaven in Hades, the underworld, where he will possess Cleopatra beyond death, and they two will rule kingdoms beyond this world. They will acquire a delightful energy, a 'sprightly port' which will astonish the other ghosts in the underworld, demoting Dido and Aeneas, formerly the greatest of the classical doomed lovers:

> Where souls do couch on flowers, we'll hand in hand
> And with our sprightly port make the ghost gaze:
> Dido and her Aeneas shall want troops,
> And all the haunt be ours.
>
> (IV.xiv.51–54)

Cleopatra 'dies' to enjoy eternal erotic pleasures with her Antony, embracing death as 'a lover's pinch / which hurts, and is desired'. Paradoxically, she poisons herself by suckling the asp, the 'baby' at her breast, the nurturing image perhaps implying that to die is to live. Her 'immortal longings' are finally satisfied. Indeed, at the end of the play, Caesar concludes the hyperbole, stating 'No grave upon the earth shall clip in it / A pair so famous'. They are united, by their suicides, in death's embrace.

Shakespeare's young lovers' death is predestined; 'a pair of star-cross'd lovers take their life'. Their love is 'death-marked'; its progress, or passage, 'fearful'. Romeo has an ominous sense of tragic destiny 'yet hanging in the stars' which will end his life, but he is willing to submit to fate: 'Let He who hath the steerage of my course / Direct my sail'. At this early stage in the play, 'He' could be divine providence, or in the Petrarchan convention, the god of love, Amor. But, at the end, when Romeo is about to take his own life, the sailing image, linked to 'passage', acquires tragic overtones. (In the literature of love, the sea – whether journeying on the sea, the waves breaking on the shore, or storms at sea – may be read as a metaphor for passion and sexual love.) 'He', the pilot of the ship, is Death:

> Come, bitter conduct, come, unsavoury guide!
> Thou desperate pilot, now at once run on
> The dashing rocks thy seasick weary bark …
>
> (V.iii.116–118)

Romeo has obliterated himself in and through love ('Thus with a kiss I die') but Juliet has a different view of their destiny. As she waits for Romeo to come to her bedroom to consummate the marriage, she plays with the certainty that death awaits her:

> Give me my Romeo, and when I shall die,
> Take him and cut him out in little stars,
> And he will make the face of heaven so fine
> That all the world will be in love with night
> And pay no worship to the garish sun.   (III.ii.21–25)

Instead of being 'star-crossed lovers' she interprets this phrase literally, with the result that they themselves ultimately control their fate and become the stars. Romeo will illuminate the darkness of the heavens when *she* has died. There is a generosity here, a willingness to share Romeo with the world in a blaze of stars. The monosyllabic lines anticipate her childish galaxy of tiny stars. Her words come true, as the Prince's closing lines to the whole play echo Juliet's endearing habit of personifying her world. The world, which was so alive for Juliet, refuses to 'play' after her death: 'The sun for sorrow will not show his head.'

A memorial to these doomed lovers is raised at the end by their grieving parents, but the question remains as to whether it was their destiny to die, so that the quarrelling households, the Capulets and Montagues, could be finally reconciled.

► Did they have to die, in order to bring peace? Does Shakespeare present the love of Romeo and Juliet as ultimately selfish or sacrificial?

Love and betrayal

'She walked rapidly in the thin June sunlight towards the worst horror of all.' These concluding lines of Graham Greene's (1904–1991) *Brighton Rock* (1938) confirm to the reader that Rose's 'undying' love for Pinkie is about to be cruelly betrayed. In this novel suicide divides, unlike *Romeo and Juliet*. Rose remains alive, her husband Pinkie having killed himself; 'withdrawn suddenly by a hand out of any existence – past or present, whipped away into zero – nothing'.

In some ways *Brighton Rock* is a macabre parody of *Romeo and Juliet*. Set in the criminal underworld of Brighton in the 1930s, it is the story of two rival gangs, of a murder which misfires, and of the marriage of two teenagers, culminating in one suicide. Both Pinkie and Rose raise memorials of their love to each other: Rose in the form of a note, Pinkie by recording his voice for Rose on a gramophone.

But this is as far as the analogy can safely stretch. Pinkie is a teenage gang leader who has committed a brutal murder. He courts and marries Rose, a young waitress, who has witnessed a crucial flaw in his defence, in order to buy her silence safely. Pinkie has many literary precedents; he is a demonic lover, a Faust who has sold his soul to the devil, whereas Rose appears to be the epitome of trusting goodness, worshipping Pinkie unquestioningly: 'Again, he got the sense that she completed him.' What they have in common is their Catholicism, their understanding of what it is to be damned or to be saved, the same worldview – and of course their visual 'colour' names, Pinkie and Rose, matching both the cinematic aspects of the novel, and also suggesting symbolically their youth tinged with blood.

It is Rose who first betrays Pinkie in that she does not put the gun to her head at the end as instructed: 'To throw away the gun was a betrayal; it would be an act of cowardice: it would mean that she chose never to see him again for ever. She put the gun up to her ear and put it down with a feeling of sickness – it was a poor love that was afraid to die.' Pinkie's betrayal of Rose occurs throughout the novel. He does not love her. He constantly feigns affection: 'He wanted to strike her, to make her scream, but he kissed her inexpertly, missing her lips.' But he is, despite himself, moved by her goodness, as he is moved, unwillingly, by music.

▶ Compare the two extracts from *Brighton Rock* in Part 3 (pages 95–96). In what ways is the second extract 'the worst horror of all'?

▶ In your reading of the literature of love, what part do letters play as a structural / narrative device?

Love and betrayal in Thomas Hardy

Thomas Hardy (1840–1928) certainly features love and betrayal in his novels and poems. The destinies of his characters are often shaped by the ironies of life, whether in the form of letters which never should have been sent, letters pushed under a door and never read, missed rendezvous, unfortunate mis-timings and coincidences, or the cruel hand of fate.

But the most extraordinary act of betrayal, coming as it were, as a *coup de théâtre* in the first act of the novel, is the wife sale at the beginning of *The Mayor of Casterbridge* (1886). The narrator at first unsettles the reader by describing the couple walking together, but separately, towards the hiring fair outside Casterbridge, with an atmosphere of 'stale familiarity'. We might assume that husband and wife have been married for years, but in fact they are young, in their early twenties. By the end of the day, the drunken and disillusioned young Michael Henchard will have sold his wife at an auction. Hardy's early poem 'Neutral Tones' (1867) had already depicted the stale end of a dead love, emphasised by the pathetic fallacy, and the same tone of *ennui*, world-weariness:

> Your eyes on me were as eyes that rove
> Over tedious riddles of years ago;

And some words played between us to and fro
On which lost the more by our love.

Again he tricks the reader into believing that the speaker has been trapped in an unhappy relationship for years. But this poem was written when Hardy was twenty-seven, almost the same age as the young Michael Henchard. The former lovers are static, dulled into stunned incomprehension that they could ever have loved each other: 'We stood by a pond that winter day'. Movement, speech, and loving looks have vanished. It is a feature of much of Hardy's writing that characters are journeying from place to place, in search of a new destiny. Yet in the poem their life together has ended here, at this place and at this moment in time, this winter day.

Here, for comparison are some key examples of betrayal and loss in Hardy's fiction:

- Henchard drinks heavily at the fair, sells his wife and child to a sailor for five guineas and subsequently must atone for his act of betrayal. The sailor Newson, however, returns at the end as a figure of Nemesis to claim justice, his own daughter Elizabeth-Jane.

- In *Far From the Madding Crowd* Fanny Robin is jilted at the altar steps by Captain Troy, having mistaken the church. She subsequently dies a wretched pauper's death, in childbirth.

- In the same novel, the flirtatious Bathsheba betrays an innocent man's love by sending a valentine to Farmer Boldwood.

- In *Tess of the D'Urbervilles* Tess and Angel's idyllic pastoral love comes to a shocking end on their wedding night, because the letter that Tess wrote, confessing her previous seduction and dead illegitimate baby, Sorrow, remains hidden under the door. Like Fanny, Tess is abandoned and betrayed.

The destinies of both Fanny and Tess owe something to the narrative structure of traditional ballads. A maiden is seduced and then forsaken, left with an illegitimate child. Claire Tomalin, in *Thomas Hardy, The Time-torn Man* (2005), writes:

> It is noticeable that when he wrote fictional accounts of country girls seduced and pregnant, he made Fanny Robin and Tess into romantic figures and victims, betrayed by men of higher social standing and driven to unhappiness and death. He made their babies die too.

Tess, broken and in despair of Angel's ever returning, allows herself to be a 'kept' woman by her former seducer, Alec d'Urberville. But fate dictates that Angel returns to claim Tess when it is 'too late'. Tess sees Angel 'dying … he looks as if he is dying! And my sin will kill him and not kill me! O, you have torn my life all to pieces … made me a victim … a caged bird!' Love and death truly meet at the moment when Tess stabs Alec, and the blood seeps down to the ceiling below, forming 'a gigantic ace of hearts'. For her crime of passion, Tess is hunted down and finally arrested while sleeping as a sacrificial victim on the altar stone at Stonehenge. She is duly sentenced to be hanged.

As a boy Thomas Hardy had been present at the hanging of Martha Browne in 1856, as he later wrote in a letter to Lady Pinney (20th January, 1926):

> I am ashamed to say I saw her hanged, my only excuse being that I was but a youth, and had to be in town at the time for other reasons. I remember what a fine figure she showed against the sky as she hung in the misty rain, and how the tight black silk gown set off her shape as she wheeled half-round and back.
>
> (quoted in Claire Tomalin *Thomas Hardy, The Time-torn Man*)

The hanging of Tess is therefore never described, nor is her time in prison. In true ballad convention, the black flag is raised at the moment of her death, watched by Angel Clare and Tess's sister Liza Lu, 'the drooping of their heads being that of Giotto's apostles' – the image suggesting that they are in fact witnesses to a crucifixion. Hardy concludes the novel as follows:

> 'Justice' was done, and the President of the Immortals (in Aeschylean phrase) had ended his sport with Tess. … The two speechless gazers bent themselves down to the earth, as if in prayer, and remained thus a long time, absolutely motionless: the flag continued to wave silently. As soon as they had strength they arose, joined hands again, and went on.

Tess has paid the ultimate price for her continued betrayal at the hands of the men in her life. Within this paragraph Hardy presents to the reader two co-existing worldviews. Tess, the victim, is no more than a pawn in the hands of an unfeeling Deity, whereas the devastated survivors, Angel and Liza Lu, derive consolation by continuing to exist, almost as Adam and Eve leaving Paradise after the Fall, in a Christian, post-lapsarian world.

▶ Tess has committed a murder. To what extent do you consider that Hardy relieves her of any moral responsibility by painting her as a victim of cruel fate?

Love, absence and death

How do the living remember the dead in the literature of love? Even an absence, a parting, a separation, is an image of death, a *memento mori*. The poet Ted Hughes, writing to his wife, Sylvia Plath, on 6th October 1956, laments his inability to focus in her absence:

> Dearest Sylvia,
> Saturday night, and no letter from my ponk. Is she dead? Has half the world dropped off?
>   This morning I could work up absolutely no interest in my stupid play, nor had I spirit for anything else. Yesterday I felt like writing but today – blank. I have read somewhere in Freud that when a person is suddenly deprived of someone he loves and has built into his life, his working powers often fail temporarily, though I should have thought they would be stimulated. I read a bit, dawdled a bit, and finally went out with my Yeats intending to read on the moor. I went up to where it was luminous that evening, and there I sat reading Yeats aloud until I was frozen and my fingers were numb. Then I set off walking in the opposite direction to back home, and followed the skyline all the way around …

Tender and affectionate intimacy, a shared literary and cultural heritage, and a desire to shape a narrative purpose to his day – to tell his story – are all present here, but the overwhelming impression is that of loss. To compensate for an emotional 'numbness', he reads Yeats until he is physically frozen. The moors provide romantic consolation: they are 'luminous'. This letter was written to someone very much alive, but absent, and despite the self-deprecating humour, Hughes here rehearses within a literary context the stages of grief the bereaved may experience.

In 1998, forty-two years later, Ted Hughes published *Birthday Letters*, poems addressed to Sylvia, dead for thirty-five years. These poems trace their courtship, marriage, the birth of their two children and the horror of Sylvia's suicide. However, comparing the above letter with any one of the *Birthday Letters,* we find a significant difference. Sylvia is his audience in 1956; he is writing for her, privately, and therefore must conjure up, in her mind, a vivid image of his day – his thoughts, his mental state, his physical activity. Thus 'I' is repeated ten times. He impresses himself upon her consciousness. But in every poem in *Birthday Letters,* it is 'you' that is resonant. The absent, lost Sylvia is resurrected through poetry. The audience is both the dead Sylvia and anonymous readers, after publication. For instance, this is the moment Ted and Sylvia make love in London in '18 Rugby Street':

> There we were.
> You were slim and lithe and smooth as a fish.
> You were a new world. My new world.
> So this is America, I marvelled.
> Beautiful, beautiful America!

He exploits the wonder of discovering the body of an American girl, whilst relishing the **intertextual** link to John Donne's 'To His Mistress Going to Bed' (see page 33, above). Later in the sequence, he describes returning to the empty house they had shared together in Devon, after a twelve-hour drive 'over the snow' down the A30 in December 1962. Here are the last two stanzas of 'Robbing Myself':

> The house made newly precious to me
> By your last lonely weeks there, and your crying,
> But sweet with cleanliness,
> Tight as a plush-lined casket
> In a safe
> In the December dusk. And, shuttered by wintering boughs,
> The stained church-windows glowed
> As if the sun had sunk there, inside the church.
>
> I listened, as I sealed it up from myself
> (The twelve-hour ice-crawl ahead).
> I peered awhile, as through the keyhole,
> Into my darkened, hushed, safe casket
> From which (I did not know)
> I had already lost the treasure.

This is profoundly elegiac writing. Timing is significant. Hughes describes his fleeting return to an empty house, which he had shared with Sylvia. Less than three months after this visit, she was to take her own life, in frozen London. Even the twelve-hour ice-crawl back to London lying 'ahead' of him is a journey towards impending death, yet without his foreknowledge.

However, as Hughes writes, so many years afterwards, his agony is transmuted into tender sorrow. Sylvia's distress is felt and addressed directly: 'your last lonely weeks there, and your crying', and there is a loving acknowledgment of her domestic skills, 'sweet with cleanliness'. Her entombment and burial is prefigured in the lexis – the house 'as tight as a plush-lined casket'. Both the month and the time of day ('December dusk') symbolise death. Hughes explicitly uses religious imagery. The church windows glow as if the sun had set, within the church. The light has gone from his home; the hearth extinguished, but gloriously, and impossibly, the sun burns within the church. Sylvia, his treasure is lost, the parenthesis – '(I did not know)' – highlighting his ignorance, his lack of complete understanding at the time, but the miraculous image of light within the church offers consolation. The church will embrace its dead. But his loss and his clumsy desolation are evidenced in the final stanza. He can no longer address Sylvia as 'you'. Alone, in his ignorance he 'peers' into a darkness, which he cannot read.

The modernist novel *To the Lighthouse* (1927) by Virginia Woolf, this 'dark book of loss and grief', was partly written to heal the grief Virginia felt at her mother's early death, Mrs Ramsay being partially based on Virginia Woolf's mother. Here is the moment when the reader first hears of her death:

> [Mr Ramsay stumbling along a passage stretched his arms out one dark morning, but Mrs Ramsay having died rather suddenly the night before, he stretched his arms out. They remained empty.]

Like Hughes, Mr Ramsay 'stumbles'. Death is presented in parenthesis, as an adjunct to life, as time separate and apart, but yet contained within the brackets – although, ironically, Mr Ramsay's enfolding arms remain empty. As in Hughes' *Birthday Letters*, here Virginia Woolf depicts the holiday house on Skye, which the Ramsay family had shared, summer after summer, now standing empty:

> how once the looking-glass had held a face; had held a world hollowed out in which a figure turned, a hand flashed, the door opened, in came children rushing and tumbling; and went out again. Now, day after day, light turned, like a flower reflected in water, its clear image on the wall outside.

This passage may be read as a microcosm of the stages of grief to be seen in the elegy. First nature feels the loss, seen in the shifting light, the absence of images in the looking glass, and also, in *Birthday Letters*, in the entombing image of the sun. Through time, 'day after day', life reasserts itself, nature providing the consolation that life is both mutable and eternal. The reflection is always present. The flower is 'reflected in water'. The measured, sequential cadences offer comfort. As Sir Michael Tippett wrote at the end of his oratorio *A Child of Our Time*:

> The moving waters renew the earth
> It is spring.

The love elegy

Two of the most significant elegy sequences in the literature of love are *In Memoriam* by Alfred Lord Tennyson, and Thomas Hardy's poems of 1912–1913. Tennyson's close university friend Arthur Hallam died on 15th September 1833: 'a blood vessel near the brain had suddenly burst'. Tennyson began writing in October that year, not publishing the poems (anonymously) until May 1850. The poems are written in four line stanzas, octosyllabics rhyming *abba*, the uniformity of rhythm and rhyme being described by the poet himself in an early poem as 'the sad mechanical exercise / Like dull narcotics, numbing pain'. Tennyson did not initially write for publication, 'until I found I had written so many. The different moods of sorrow as in a drama are dramatically given, and my conviction that fear, doubts and suffering will find answer and relief only through Faith in a God of Love.' The poems were a source of comfort to Queen Victoria on the death of her consort Prince Albert; indeed, they helped gain Tennyson the Poet Laureateship.

Thomas Hardy's wife, Emma Gifford, died suddenly from heart failure on 27th November 1912 at the age of 72. Her death disturbed him profoundly and prompted him to atone for his prolonged neglect of her by a passionate outpouring of elegiac love poetry, with every single poem subtly different in form. Hardy wrote in a letter to Edward Clodd (13th December, 1912):

> One forgets all the recent years and differences and the mind goes back to the early times when each was much to the other – in her case and mine intensely much.
>
> (quoted in Claire Tomalin *Thomas Hardy, The Time-torn Man*)

He recaptures the days of their courtship in Cornwall, almost fifty years earlier, and recalls her vibrant spirit – the way her vitality made luminous every place they visited: 'the waterfall, above which the mist-bow shone / At the then fair hour in the then fair weather' ('After a Journey'). But the shock of her absence is felt in the present too. Tennyson had stated (in poem V) that the act of writing poetry as a means of expressing grief is a guilty comfort, a protection against the cold like a comfort blanket, but that any attempt to express the sorrow in mere words must only be in outline. In Hardy's poem 'The Walk', the degree of raw pain the poet is experiencing is in direct proportion to the simplicity of the diction. Recently, Emma had been too lame to accompany Hardy on his customary walk to the hill-top tree. Here is the second stanza:

> I walked up there today
> Just in the former way;
> > Surveyed around
> > The familiar ground
> > By myself again:
> > What difference, then?
> Only that underlying sense
> Of the look of a room on returning thence.

▶ Compare Hardy's return to his home with the extract from Ted Hughes' 'Robbing Myself' (page 74, above). What is the effect of understatement here?

3 | Texts and extracts

The texts and extracts which follow have been chosen to illustrate points made elsewhere in the book, and to provide material which may be useful when working on assignments. The sequence of the texts and extracts matches their appearance in Parts 1 and 2.

William Cartwright

'No Platonique Love'

William Cartwright (1611–1643) was a Royalist, a follower of Charles I. He was also a successful playwright, as seen by the dramatic, conversational qualities of this poem, which challenge the listener's preconceptions about 'platonic' love. All spellings are original.

> Tell me no more of minds embracing minds,
> And hearts exchang'd for hearts;
> That Spirits Spirits meet, as Winds do Winds,
> And mix their subt'lest parts;
> That two unbodi'd Essences may kiss,
> And then, like Angels, twist and feel one Bliss.
>
> I was that silly thing that once was wrought
> To practise this thin Love;
> I climbed from Sex to Soul, from Soul to Thought,
> But thinking there to move,
> Headlong, I rowl'd from Thought to Soul, and then
> From Soul I lighted at the Sex agen.
>
> As some strict down-look'd men pretend to fast
> Who yet in Closets Eat;
> So Lovers who profess they Spirits taste,
> Feed yet on grosser meat;
> I know they boast they Soules to Soules Convey,
> How e'er they meet, the Body is the Way.
>
> Come, I will undeceive thee, they that tread
> Those vain Aeriall waies,
> Are like young Heyrs, and Alchymists misled
> To waste their wealth and Daies,
> For searching thus to be for ever Rich,
> They only find a Med'cine for the Itch.

John Donne

'Negative Love'

The *Songs and Sonets* of John Donne (1572–1631) is a collection of love poems, varying greatly in both tone and content, from the tender to the salacious. Consciously male poems, at times misogynistic, they inform the reader that this is how a man loves. 'Negative Love' is measured, progressing through platonic stages of love to the point where meaning vanishes. Only the 'negative' may define this refined love. John Donne was also a priest and theologian, and this poem marks the interface between love and theology.

> I never stoop'd so low, as they
> Which on an eye, cheek, lip, can prey;
> Seldom to them, which soar no higher
> Than virtue, or the mind to admire.
> For sense, and understanding may
> Know what gives fuel to their fire:
> My love, though silly, is more brave,
> For may I miss, whene'er I crave,
> If I know yet, what I would have.
>
> If that be simply perfectest,
> Which can by no way be express'd
> But negatives, my love is so.
> To All, which all love, I say no.
> If any who deciphers best,
> What we know not, ourselves, can know,
> Let him teach me that nothing; This
> As yet my ease and comfort is,
> Though I speed not, I cannot miss.

John Milton

From *Paradise Lost* Book 9 (1667)

Milton's (1608–1674) epic poem *Paradise Lost*, as the title suggests, narrates the loss of Paradise, the expulsion of Adam and Eve from the Garden of Eden. Satan, disguised as a snake, tempts Eve to eat from the Tree of Knowledge. Fully aware that this was expressly forbidden by God, out of love for Eve Adam nevertheless follows her in eating the apple. This event, known as the Fall, causes cataclysmic disturbances both on a cosmic and human level. The world physically shifts on its axis from perfect harmony to change, mutability and corruption. Death enters the world, and men and women may no longer reside in Paradise, but must endure hardship, suffering and death in a hostile world. Adam and Eve's innocent existence before the Fall was termed pre-lapsarian; all the subsequent events, post-lapsarian. The first extract describes the very moment of the Fall; the second, Adam's horrified response.

1   So saying, her rash hand in evil hour
    Forth reaching to the fruit, she plucked, she ate:
    Earth felt the wound, and nature from her seat
    Sighing through all her works gave signs of woe,
    That all was lost. Back to the thicket slunk
    The guilty serpent, and well might, for Eve
    Intent now wholly on her taste, naught else
    Regarded, such delight till then, as seemed,
    In fruit she never tasted, whether true
    Or fancied so, through expectation high
    Of knowledge, nor was godhead from her thought.
    Greedily she engorged without restraint,
    And knew not eating death: satiate at length,
    And heightened as with wine, jocund and boon,
    Thus to herself she pleasingly began:

2   From his slack hand the garland wreathed for Eve
    Down dropped, and all the faded roses shed:
    Speechless he stood and pale, till thus at length
    First to himself he inward silence broke …

    'How art thou lost, how on a sudden lost,
    Defaced, deflowered, and now to death devote!
    Rather how hast thou yielded to transgress
    The strict forbiddance, how to violate
    The sacred fruit forbidden! Some cursed fraud
    Of enemy hath beguiled thee, yet unknown,
    And me with thee hath ruined, for with thee
    Certain my resolution is to die;
    How can I live without thee, how forgo
    Thy sweet converse and love so dearly joined,
    To live again in these wild woods forlorn?
    Should God create another Eve, and I
    Another rib afford, yet loss of thee
    Would never from my heart; no, no, I feel
    The link of nature draw me: flesh of my flesh,
    Bone of my bone thou art, and from thy state
    Mine never shall be parted, bliss or woe.

The Bible: King James Version

From *Song of Songs*, Chapter 2

1   I am the rose of Sharon and the lily of the valleys.

2   As the lily among thorns, so is my love among the daughters.

3   As the apple tree among the trees in the wood, so is my beloved among the sons. I sat down under his shadow with great delight, and his fruit was sweet to my taste.

4   He brought me to the banqueting house, and his banner over me was love.

5   Stay me with flagons, comfort me with apples: for I am sick of love.

6   His left hand is under my head, and his right hand doth embrace me.

7   I charge you, o ye daughters of Jerusalem, by the roes, and by the hinds of the fields, that ye stir not up, nor wake my love, till he please.

8   The voice of my beloved! Behold, he cometh leaping upon the mountains, skipping upon the hills.

9   My beloved is like a roe or a young hart: behold, he standeth behind our wall, he looketh forth at the windows, shewing himself through the lattice.

10 My beloved spake, and said unto me, Rise up, my love, my fair one, and come away.

11 For, lo, the winter is past, the rain is over and gone;

12 The flowers appear on the earth; the time of the singing of birds is come, and the voice of the turtle is heard in the land …

16 My beloved is mine, and I am his: he feedeth among the lilies.

17 Until the day break, and the shadows flee away, turn, my beloved, and be thou like a roe or a young hart upon the mountain of Bether.

Edmund Spenser

From 'Epithalamion' (1595)

Edmund Spenser (1552–1599) was the most prolific poet of his age. His longest poem is *The Faerie Queene,* an Arthurian epic written in honour of the noble virtues of Queen Elizabeth, Gloriana. He married Elizabeth Boyle in 1594, having courted her with his sonnet sequence *Amoretti* (little loves). This extract from 'Epithalamion', the wedding song, marks the arrival of the bride.

Loe where she comes along with portly pace,
Lyke Phoebe from her chamber of the East,
Arysing forth to run her mighty race,
Clad all in white, that seemes a virgin best.
So well it her beseemes that ye would weene
Some angell she had beene.
Her long loose yellow locks lyke golden wyre,
Sprinckled with perle, and perling flowres a tweene,
Doe like a golden mantle her attyre,
And being crowned with a girland greene,
Seeme lyke some mayden Queene.
Her modest eyes abashed to behold
So many gazers, as on her do stare,
Upon the lowly ground affixed are.
Ne dare lift up her countenance too bold,
But blush to heare her praises sung so loud,
So farre from being proud.
Nathlesse doe ye still loud her praises sing,
That all the woods may answer and your eccho ring.

Tell me, ye merchants daughters, did ye see
So fayre a creature in your towne before?
So sweet, so lovely, and so mild as she,
Adorned with beautyes grace and virtues store?
Her goodly eyes lyke Saphyres shining bright,
Her forehead yvory white,
Her cheekes like apples which the sun hath rudded,
Her lips like cherries charming men to byte,
Her brest like to a bowl of creame uncrudded,
Her paps lyke lillies budded,
Her snowie neck like to a marble towre,
And all her body lyke a pallace fayre,
Ascending uppe with many a stately stayre,
To honors seat and chastities sweet bowre.
Why stand ye still, ye virgins, in amaze,
Upon her so to gaze,
Whiles ye forget your former lay to sing,
To which the woods did answer and your eccho ring?

Alexander Pope

From *Eloisa to Abelard* (1717)

Pope (1688–1744) published *Eloisa to Abelard* in 1717. In the 12th century, Eloisa fell in love with her teacher, Peter Abelard, a distinguished theologian. However, they were discovered and separated, never to meet again. This extract, from her imagined letter to him, voices her 'unholy passion'. She is not content to be imprisoned as a devout nun.

'How happy is the blameless Vestal's lot!
The world forgetting, by the world forgot.
Eternal sunshine of the spotless mind!
Each prayer accepted, and each wish resign'd;

****

Far other dreams my erring soul employ,
Far other rapture, of unholy joy;
When at the close of each sad, sorrowing day,
Fancy restores what vengeance snatched away,
Then conscience sleeps, and leaving nature free,
All my loosed soul unbounded springs to thee.
O curst, dear horrors of all-conscious night!
How glowing guilt exalts the keen delight!
Provoking Dæmons all restraint remove,
And stir within me ev'ry source of love.
I hear thee, view thee, gaze o'er all thy charms,
And round thy phantom glue my clasping arms.
I wake: – no more I hear, no more I view,
The phantom flies me, as unkind as you.
I call aloud; it hears not what I say:
I stretch my empty arms; it glides away.
To dream once more I close my willing eyes;
Ye soft illusions, dear deceits, arise;
Alas, no more! Methinks we wandering go
Through dreary wastes, and weep each other's woe,
Where, round some mouldering tower, pale ivy creeps,
And low-brow'd rocks hang nodding o'er the deeps,
Sudden you mount, you beckon from the skies;
Clouds interpose, waves roar, and winds arise.
I shriek, start up, the same sad prospect find,
And wake to all the griefs I left behind.'

THE LITERATURE OF LOVE

Robert Herrick

'To the Virgins, to Make Much of Time'

Herrick (1591–1674) has been described as one of the finest English lyric poets. Priest, Royalist and poet, he was buried in an unmarked grave in Dean Prior, Devonshire. His poetry and his reputation, though much admired up to the beginning of the First World War, have been eclipsed by the precedence given since then to Herrick's contemporaries, the Metaphysical Poets.

> Gather ye rosebuds while ye may,
>   Old time is still a-flying;
> And this same flower that smiles today
>   Tomorrow will be dying.
>
> The glorious lamp of heaven, the sun,
>   The higher he's a-getting,
> The sooner will his race be run,
>   And nearer he's to setting.
>
> That age is best which is the first,
>   When youth and blood are warmer,
> But being spent, the worse, and worst
>   Times still succeed the former.
>
> Then be not coy, but use your time,
>   And, while ye may, go marry:
> For, having lost but once your prime.
>   You may for ever tarry.

W.H. Auden

'Alone' (1941)

A major 20th-century poet, Auden (1907–1973) gained many international awards for his poetry. His influence on successive generations of poets was immense. Anglo Catholic, homosexual and politically active, much of his poetry mines the relationship between love, fidelity and death. 'O Tell me the Truth about Love', 'Lullaby', and 'Stop all the Clocks' are famous, thanks in part to exposure in the film *Four Weddings and a Funeral*. 'Alone', written in the USA, is a **villanelle** in form, as is the more famous 'If I could tell You'.

> Each lover has a theory of his own
> About the difference between the ache
> Of being with his love, and being alone:

Why what, when dreaming, is dear flesh and bone
That really stirs the senses, when awake,
Appears a simulacrum of his own.

Narcissus disbelieves in the unknown;
He cannot join his image in the lake
So long as he assumes he is alone.

The child, the waterfall, the fire, the stone,
Are always up to mischief, though, and take
The universe for granted as their own.

The elderly, like Proust, are always prone
To think of love as a subjective fake;
The more they love, the more they feel alone.

Whatever view we hold, it must be shown
Why every lover has a wish to make
Some other kind of otherness his own:
Perhaps, in fact, we never are alone.

Geoffrey Chaucer

From *Troilus and Criseyde*

Set in the Trojan wars, *Troilus and Criseyde* is Chaucer's (1343–1400) own
epic poem. Troilus falls in love with Criseyde; she is willing to become his lover.
However, she is soon unfaithful. This 'Canticus Troili' or 'Song of Troilus' occurs
near the beginning of the poem. He is tormented by a thing called love.

If no love is, O God, what fele I so?
And if love is, what thing and which is he?
If love be good, from whennes cometh my wo?   (*whennes* whence)
If it be wikke, a wonder thynketh me,   (*wikke* evil)
Whan every torment and adversite
That cometh of him may to me savory thinke,   (*savory thinke* seem
For ay thurst I, the more that ich it drynke.   pleasant)

And if that at myn owen lust I brenne,   (*brenne* burn)
From whennes cometh my waillynge and my pleynte?   (*pleynte*
If harm agree me, wherto pleyne I thenne?   complaint)
I noot, ne whi unwery that I feynte.   (*I noot* I do not know)
O quikke deth, O swete harm so queynte,
How may of the in me swich quantite,
But if that I consente that it be?

And if that I consente, I wrongfully
Compleyne, iwis. Thus possed to and fro,   (*iwis* indeed)
Al stereless within a boot am I   (*stereless* rudderless; *boot* boat)
Amydde the see, bitwixen wyndes two,
That in contrarie stonden evere mo.
Allas, what is this wondre maladie?
For hete of cold, for cold of hete I die.

Lady Mary Wroth

from *Pamphilia to Amphilanthus* (1621)

Lady Mary Wroth (1587–1651) was the niece of Sir Philip Sidney (see page 88, below). After the death of her husband, Sir Robert Wroth, she took the Earl of Pembroke as her lover. This sonnet comes from her Petrarchan sonnet sequence, *Pamphilia to Amphilanthus* (the 'all loving' to 'he who loves two'). The names suggest adultery.

Late in the forest I did Cupid see
Cold, wett, and crying he had lost his way,
And being blind was farder like to stray:
Which sight a kind compassion bred in me,

I kindly tooke, and dride him, while that he
Poore child complain'd he sterved was with stay,
And pin'de fro want of his accustom'd pray,
For non in that wilde place his hoste would bee,

I glad was of his finding, thinking sure
This service should my freedome still procure,
and in my armes I took him then unharmde,

Carrying him safe unto a Mirtle bowre
Butt in the way he made mee feele his powre,
burning my hart who had him kindly warmd.

E.E. Cummings

'somewhere I have never travelled, gladly beyond' (1931)

E.E. Cummings (1894–1962) was an American poet, Harvard educated. He was influenced by the English Romantic poets, and his own poems convey a tender lyricism, exposed by his original typography, using only lower-case letters.

somewhere i have never travelled, gladly beyond
any experience, your eyes have their silence:
in your most frail gesture are things which enclose me,
or which i cannot touch because they are too near

your slightest look easily will unclose me
though i have closed myself as fingers,
you open always petal by petal myself as Spring opens
(touching skilfully, mysteriously) her first rose

or if your wish be to close me, i and
my life will shut very beautifully, suddenly,
as when the heart of this flower imagines
the snow carefully everywhere descending;

nothing which we are to perceive in this world equals
the power of your intense fragility: whose texture
compels me with the colour of its countries,
rendering death and forever with each breathing

(i do not know what it is about you that closes
and opens; only something in me understands
the voice of your eyes is deeper than all roses)
nobody, not even the rain has such small hands

William Shakespeare

From *Othello* (1604)

Othello is a tragedy of a murderous domestic love. At this point in the play (Act 5)
Othello has smothered his wife, Desdemona. Emilia discovers the horrific scene:

EMILIA:	Help, help, ho, help! O, lady, speak again!
	Sweet Desdemona, O sweet mistress, speak!
DESDEMONA:	A guiltless death I die.
EMILIA:	O, who hath done this deed?
DESDEMONA:	Nobody; I myself. Farewell.
	Commend me to my kind lord. O farewell *She dies*
OTHELLO:	Why, how should she be murdered?
EMILIA:	Alas, who knows?
OTHELLO:	You heard her say herself it was not I.
EMILIA:	She said so; I must needs report the truth.
OTHELLO:	She's like a liar gone to burning hell:
	'Twas I that killed her.
EMILIA:	O, the more angel she,
	And you the blacker devil!
OTHELLO:	She turned to folly, and she was a whore.
EMILIA:	Thou dost belie her, and thou art a devil.
OTHELLO:	She was as false as water.
EMILIA:	Thou art rash as fire to say
	That she was false. O, she was heavenly true!

Emily Brontë

From *Wuthering Heights* (1847)

Wuthering Heights tells of the passionate relationship, never consummated, between Catherine Earnshaw and Heathcliff. Here, Cathy is dying, but her heart's desire is to be embraced by the man she truly loves, Heathcliff.

With straining eagerness Catherine gazed towards the entrance of her chamber. He did not hit the right room directly; she motioned me to admit him; but he found it out, ere I could reach the door, and in a stride or two was at her side, and had her grasped in his arms.

He neither spoke, nor loosed his hold, for some five minutes, during which period he bestowed more kisses than he ever gave in his life before, I dare say; but then my mistress had kissed him first, and I plainly saw that he could hardly bear, for downright agony, to look into her face! The same conviction had stricken him as me, from the instant he beheld her, that there was no prospect of ultimate recovery there – she was fated, sure to die.

'Oh, Cathy! Oh, my life! How can I bear it?' was the first sentence he uttered, in a tone that did not seek to disguise his despair.

And now he stared at her so earnestly that I thought the very intensity of his gaze would bring tears into his eyes; but they burned with anguish, they did not melt.

'What now?' said Catherine, leaning back, and returning his look with a suddenly clouded brow – her humour was a mere vane for constantly varying caprices. 'You and Edgar have broken my heart, Heathcliff! And you both come to bewail the deed to me, as if you were the people to be pitied! I shall not pity you, not I. You have killed me – and thriven on it, I think. How strong you are! How many years do you mean to live after I am gone?'

Heathcliff had knelt on one knee to embrace her; he attempted to rise, but she seized his hair, and kept him down.

'I wish I could hold you,' she continued, bitterly, 'till we were both dead! I shouldn't care what you suffered. I care nothing for your sufferings. Why shouldn't you suffer? I do! Will you forget me – will you be happy when I am in the earth? Will you say twenty years hence, 'That's the grave of Catherine Earnshaw. I loved her long ago, and was wretched to lose her, but it is past. I've loved many others since – my children are dearer to me than she was, and at death, I shall not rejoice that I am going to her, I shall be sorry that I must leave them!' Will you say so, Heathcliff?'

'Don't torture me till I'm as mad as yourself,' cried he, wrenching his head free, and grinding his teeth.

The two, to a cool spectator, made a strange and fearful picture. Well might Catherine deem that heaven would be a land of exile to her, unless, with her mortal body, she cast away her mortal character too. Her present countenance had a wild vindictiveness in its white cheek, and a bloodless lip, and a scintillating eye, and she retained, in her closed fingers, a portion of the locks she had been grasping. As to her companion, while raising himself with one hand, he had taken her arm with the other, and so inadequate was his stock of gentleness to the requirements of her condition, that on his letting go, I saw four distinct impressions left blue in the colourless skin.

Sir Philip Sidney

From *Astrophel and Stella*

Sir Philip Sidney (1554–1586) was the epitome of the Renaissance man – highly educated with a distinguished military and political career. His *Astrophel and Stella* began the vogue for named sonnet sequences. This Petrarchan sonnet aches with tenderness and intelligence. Questions are always rhetorical. The moon may never reply.

> With how sad steps, Oh Moon, thou climb'st the skies,
> How silently, and with how wan a face!
> What may it be, that even in heavenly place
> That busy archer his sharp arrows tries?
> Sure, if that long- with- love-acquainted eyes
> Can judge of love, thou feel'st a lover's case;
> I read it in thy looks; thy languished grace,
> To me that feel the like, thy state descries.
> Then even of fellowship, Oh Moon, tell me,
> Is constant love deemed there but want of wit?
> Are beauties there as proud as here they be?
> Do they above love to be loved, and yet
> Those lovers scorn whom that love doth possess?
> Do they call virtue there ungratefulness?

D.H. Lawrence

From *The Rainbow* (1915)

Three years before the publication of this novel, Lawrence (1885–1930) had eloped to Germany with Frieda Weekley, wife of his former German Professor. He never settled permanently in England again. His books were frequently misunderstood and misrepresented: *The Rainbow* was banned for being 'pornographic'; Penguin Books were prosecuted in 1959 for publishing *Lady Chatterley's Lover*. However, Bishop John Robinson, Bishop of Woolwich, defended it at its trial, suggesting that 'what Lawrence is trying to do is to portray the sex relationship as something essentially sacred'.

And the whole rhythm of him beat into his kisses, and still he pursued her, in his kisses, and still she was not quite overcome. He wondered over the moonlight on her nose! All the moonlight upon her, all the darkness within her! All the night in his arms, darkness and shine, he possessed of it all! All the night for him now, to unfold, to venture within, all the mystery to be entered, all the discovery to be made.

Trembling with keen triumph, his heart was as white as a star as he drove his kisses nearer.

'My love,' she called, in a low voice, from afar.

The low sound seemed to call to him from afar off, under the moon, to him who was unaware. He stopped, quivered, and listened.

And they kissed on the mouth, in rapture and surprise, long, real kisses. The kiss lasted, there among the moonlight. He kissed her again, and she kissed him. And again they were kissing together. Till something happened in him, he was strange. He wanted her. He wanted her exceedingly. She was something new …

… 'My love,' came again the low plaintive cry, like a bird unseen in the night.

He was afraid. His heart quivered and broke. He was stopped.

'Anna,' he said, as if he answered her from a distance, unsure.

'My love.'

And he drew near, and she drew near.

'Anna,' he said in wonder and birthpain of love.

'My love,' she said, her voice growing rapturous.

He held close to her hand. He was dazed and could not move, he did not know how to move. She drew him away.

He walked helplessly beside her, holding her hand. She went with bent head. Suddenly he said, as the simple solution stated itself to him:

'We'll get married, Anna.'

She was silent.

'We'll get married, Anna, shall we?'

She stopped in the field again and kissed him, clinging to him passionately, in a way he could not understand. But he left it all to marriage. That was the solution now, fixed ahead. He wanted her, he wanted to be married to her, he wanted to have her altogether, as his own for ever.

Oscar Wilde

From *The Importance of Being Earnest* (1895)

A Trivial Comedy for Serious People (as Wilde described it in the play's subtitle) was first performed on Valentine's Day, 1895 at St James's Theatre, London. A 19th-century comedy of manners, the women make the running here.

> GWENDOLEN: I adore you. But you haven't proposed to me yet. Nothing has been said at all about marriage. The subject has not even been touched on.
>
> JACK: Well – may I propose to you now?
>
> GWENDOLEN: I think it would be an admirable opportunity. And to spare you any possible disappointment, Mr Worthing, I think it only fair to tell you quite frankly beforehand that I am determined to accept you.
>
> JACK: Gwendolen!
>
> GWENDOLEN: Yes, Mr Worthing, what have you got to say to me?
>
> JACK: You know what I have got to say to you.
>
> GWENDOLEN: Yes, but you don't say it.
>
> JACK: Gwendolen, will you marry me? (*Goes on his knees*)
>
> GWENDOLEN: Of course I will, darling. How long you have been about it! I am afraid you have had very little experience in how to propose.
>
> JACK: My own one, I have never loved anyone in the world but you.
>
> GWENDOLEN: Yes, but men often propose for practice.

Evelyn Waugh

From *Vile Bodies* (1930)

Vile Bodies recounts the adventures of a fictional Mayfair set in the 'Roaring Twenties'. In the following passage, Chapter 11 in its entirety, Adam has bad news for Nina. Not a proposal, but an 'unproposal' – and third-party proposal and acceptance all take place over the telephone:

> Adam rang up Nina.
>
> 'Darling, I've been so happy about your telegram. Is it really true?'
>
> 'No, I'm afraid not.'
>
> 'The major is bogus?'
>
> 'Yes'
>
> 'You haven't got any money?'
>
> 'No.'
>
> 'I see.'
>
> 'Well?'
>
> 'I said, I see.'
>
> 'Is that all?'

'Yes, that's all, Adam.'
'I'm sorry.'
'I'm sorry, too. Goodbye.'

Later, Nina rang up Adam.
'Darling, is that you?
I've got something rather awful to tell you.'
'Yes?'
'You'll be furious.'
'Well?'
'I'm engaged to be married.'
'Who to?'
'I hardly think I can tell you.'
'Who?'
'Adam, you won't be beastly about it, will you?'
'Who is it?'
'Ginger.'
'I don't believe it.'
'Well, I am. That's all there is to it.'
'You're going to marry Ginger?'
'Yes.'
'I see.'
'Well?'
'I said, I see.'
'Is that all?'
'Yes, that's all, Nina.'
'When shall I see you?'
'I don't ever want to see you again.'
'I see.'
'Well?'
'I said, I see.'
'Well, good-bye.'
'Good-bye ... I'm sorry, Adam.'

Edward Albee

From *Who's Afraid of Virginia Woolf?* (1962)

Set in a small town American university campus, this play dissects two marriages. George and Martha are playing games with the younger couple, Nick and Honey. Here George takes centre stage, with Honey and Nick as his audience. Honey begins to grasp that the tale concerns her.

GEORGE: How They Got Married. Well, how they got married is this ... The mouse got all puffed up one day and she went over to Blondie's house, and she stuck out her puff and she said ... look at me.

HONEY: (*white ... on her feet*) I ... don't ... like this.

NICK: (*to George*) Stop it!

GEORGE: Look at me ... I'm all puffed up. Oh my goodness, said Blondie.

HONEY: (*as from a distance*) ... and so they were married.

GEORGE: ... And so they were married ...

HONEY: ... And then ...

GEORGE: ... and then.

HONEY: (*hysteria*) WHAT? and then, WHAT?

NICK: NO! no!

GEORGE: (*as if to a baby*) and then the puff went *away* ... Like magic ... pouf!

NICK: (*almost sick*) Jesus God.

HONEY: ... the puff went away ...

GEORGE: ... pouf

NICK: Honey... I didn't mean to ... honestly, I didn't mean to ...

HONEY: You ... you told them.

HONEY: (*grabbing at her belly*) Ohhhh nooooo.

NICK: Honey ... baby ... I'm sorry ... I didn't mean to.

GEORGE: (*abruptly and with some disgust*) And that's how you play Get the Guests.

Elizabeth Barrett Browning

from *Sonnets from the Portuguese* (1850)

After spending several years as an invalid, Elizabeth Barrett (1806–1861) fell in love with Robert Browning, and secretly married him. They spent the rest of their married life in Italy. Rather than declining into an isolated death as an invalid, in this poem the poet embraces the joys of married life on earth with her lover.

> Is it indeed so? If I lay here dead,
> Would'st thou miss any life in losing mine?
> And would the sun for thee more coldly shine,
> Because of grave-damps falling round my head?
> I marvelled, my Belovèd, when I read
> Thy thought so in the letter. I am thine –
> But ... *so* much to thee? Can I pour thy wine
> While my hands tremble? Then my soul, instead
> Of dreams of death, resumes life's lower range.
> Then, love me, Love! look on me ... breathe on me!
> As brighter ladies do not count it strange,
> For love, to give up acres and degree,
> I yield the grave for thy sake, and exchange
> My near sweet view of heaven, for earth with thee!

Henry James

From *The Portrait of a Lady* (1881)

This extract marks the point in the novel where Isabel Archer sees clearly that her husband does not love her. It comes as a dark epiphany.

It was as if he had had the evil eye; as if his presence were a blight and his favour a misfortune. Was it the fault in himself, or only in the deep mistrust she had conceived for him? This mistrust was now the clearest result of their short married life; a gulf had opened between them over which they looked at each other with eyes that were on either side a declaration of the deception suffered. It was a strange opposition, of the like of which she had never dreamed – an opposition in which the vital principle of the one was a thing of contempt to the other. It was not her fault – she had practised no deception; she had only admired and believed. She had taken all the first steps in the purest confidence, and then she had suddenly found the infinite vista of a multiplied life to be a dark, narrow valley with a dead wall at the end. Instead of leading to the high places of happiness, from which the worlds would seem to lie below one, so that one could look down with sense of exultation and advantage, and judge and choose and pity, it led rather downward and earthward, into the realms of restriction and depression where the sound of other lives, easier and freer, was heard as from above, and where it served to deepen the feeling of failure. It was her deep distrust of her husband – this was what darkened the world... then the shadows had begun to gather; it was as if Osmond deliberately, almost malignantly, had put the lights out one by one.

Vicki Feaver

'The Crack'

Born in Nottingham, Vicki Feaver has won many awards for her poetry. Her metaphors compel the reader; in particular, she employs classical myth in order to shed light on the female condition in dramatic monologues such as 'Medusa' and 'Circe'. This poem appears to materialise out of nowhere like a crack in the wall.

cut right though the house –
a thick, wiggly line
you could poke a finger into,
a deep gash seeping
fine black dust.

It didn't appear overnight.
For a long time
it was such a fine line
we went up and down stairs
oblivious of the stresses

that were splitting
our walls and ceilings apart.
And even when it thickened
and darkened, we went on
not seeing, or seeing

but believing the crack
would heal itself,
if dry earth was to blame,
a winter of rain
would seal its edges.

You didn't tell me
that you heard at night
its faint stirrings
like something alive.
And I didn't tell you –

until the crack
had opened so wide
that if we'd moved in our sleep
to reach for each other
we'd have fallen through.

Zora Neale Hurston

From *Their Eyes Were Watching God* (1937)

Zora Neale Hurston inspired a generation of African-American writers: Toni Morrison, Alice Walker and Maya Angelou. Oprah Winfrey calls *Their Eyes Were Watching God* her 'favourite love story of all time'. The novelist Zadie Smith has edited the Virago edition of this book. The novel tells of the two disastrous marriages Janie makes before finding happiness. In this extract Janie reflects on what her marriage to Jody has become.

> Times and scenes like that put Janie to thinking about the inside state of her marriage. Time came when she fought back with her tongue as best she could, but it didn't do her any good. It just made Joe do more. He wanted her submission and he'd keep on fighting until he felt he had it.
>
> So gradually, she pressed her teeth together and learned to hush.

THE LITERATURE OF LOVE

The spirit of the marriage left the bedroom and took to living in the parlour. It was there to shake hands whenever company came to visit, but it never went back inside the bedroom again. So she put something there to represent the spirit like a Virgin Mary image in a church. The bed was no longer a daisy-field for her and Joe to play in. It was a place where she went and lay down when she was sleepy and tired.

She wasn't petal open anymore with him. She was twenty-four and seven years married when she knew. She found that out one day when he slapped her face in the kitchen. It happened over one of those dinners that chasten all women sometimes. They plan and they fix and they do, and then some kitchen-dwelling fiend slips a scrochy, soggy, tasteless mess into their pots and pans. Janie was a good cook, and Joe had looked forward to his dinner as a refuge from other things. So when the bread didn't rise, and the fish wasn't done at the bone, and the rice was scorched, he slapped Janie until she had a ringing sound in her ears and told her about her brains before he stalked on back to the store.

Janie stood where he left her for unmeasured time and thought. She stood there until something fell off the shelf inside her. Then she went inside there to see what it was. It was her image of Jody tumbled down and shattered. But looking at it she saw that it never was the flesh and blood figure of her dreams. Just something she had grabbed up to drape her dreams over. In a way she turned her back upon the image where it lay and looked further. She had no more blossomy openings dusting pollen over her man, neither any glistening young fruit where the petals used to be. She found that she had a host of thoughts she had never expressed to him, and numerous emotions she had never let Jody know about. Things packed up and put away in parts of her heart where he could never find them. She was saving up feelings for some man she had never seen. She had an inside and an outside now and suddenly she knew how not to mix them.

Graham Greene

From *Brighton Rock* (1938)

The novel is set in gangland Brighton, in the 1930s. Pinkie, the seventeen-year-old gang leader, decides to marry Rose, a young waitress, in order to buy her silence as she has knowledge which could hang him. Both are Catholics. She falls in love with him. The first extract occurs just after their marriage, when Pinkie discovers a note in his pocket from Rose; the second when Rose requests something 'to remember him by'. He goes into a booth to make a recording of his voice.

The air was fresh like country air. He could imagine he had escaped. He put his hands for warmth into his trouser-pockets and felt a scrap of paper, which should not have been there. He drew it out – a scrap torn from a note-book – big, unformed, stranger's writing. He held it up into the grey light and read – with difficulty. 'I love you, Pinkie. I don't care what you do. I love you for ever. You've been good to me. Wherever you go, I'll go too.' He crumpled it in his fist, a dustbin stood outside a fishmonger's – then he held his hand. An obscure sense told him you never knew – it might prove useful one day.

****

He went into the box and closed the door. There was a slot for his sixpence: a mouthpiece: an instruction, 'Speak clearly and close to the instrument'. The scientific paraphernalia made him nervous. He looked over his shoulder and there outside she was watching him, without a smile. He saw her as a stranger: a shabby child from Nelson Place and he was shaken by an appalling resentment. He put in sixpence, and speaking in a low voice for fear it might carry beyond the box, he gave his message up to be graven on vulcanite: 'God damn you, you little bitch, why can't you go back home for ever and let me be?' He heard the needle scratch and the record whirr; then a click and silence.

Carrying the black disc he came out to her. 'Here,' he said, 'take it. I put something on it – loving.'

4 | Critical approaches

- How has the literature of love shaped cultural and literary history?

- How do differing critical approaches help to interpret the literature of love?

- Do different genders read the literature of love differently?

Writing in *Doing English* (2000) Robert Eaglestone informs his readers that:

> The realisation that how we read is as important as what we read is perhaps the most important innovation in the study of literature in the last twenty or thirty years. It has changed English completely as a subject and given it a new burst of life. And it is this realisation that underlies the new ways of reading that are called, in a rather all-inclusive way, 'literary theory'.

One text, he points out, may be interpreted in many different ways. Hermeneutics is the study of interpretation.

Reading *Brideshead Revisited*

The following section considers an extract from *Brideshead Revisited* (1945) by Evelyn Waugh from a variety of different critical perspectives. The extract comes towards the end of the novel. Charles Ryder, the narrator, meets Sebastian Flyte's sister, Julia, unexpectedly on an ocean liner returning from America to England. Both Charles and Julia are married, Charles to Celia, Julia to Rex. They have spent time, two days, together alone on deck while a dramatic sea storm rages, incapacitating their fellow travellers. This is the third and final day of the storm.

> Rain ceased at midday; at evening the clouds dispersed and the sun, astern of us, suddenly broke into the lounge where we sat, putting all the lights to shame.
> 'Sunset,' said Julia, 'the end of our day.'
> She rose, and though the roll and pitch of the ships seemed unabated, led me up to the boat-deck. She put her arm through mine and her hand into mine, in my great-coat pocket. The deck was dry and empty, swept only by the wind of the ship's speed. As we made our halting, laborious way forward, away from the flying smuts of the smoke stack, we were alternately jostled together, then strained, nearly sundered, arms and fingers interlocked as I held the rail, and Julia clung to me; thrust together again, drawn apart; then, in a plunge deeper than the rest, I found myself flung across her,

pressing her against the rail, warding myself off her with my arms that held her prisoner on either side, and as the ship paused at the end of its drop as though gathering strength for the ascent, we stood thus embraced, in the open cheek against cheek, her hair blowing across my eyes; the dark horizon of tumbling water, flashing now with gold, stood still above us, then came sweeping down till I was staring through Julia's dark hair in a wide and golden sky, and she was thrown forward onto my heart, held up by my hands on the rail, her face still pressed to mine.

In that minute, with her lips to my ear and her breath warm in the salt wind, Julia said, as though I had not spoken, 'Yes, now,' and as the ship righted herself and for the moment ran into calmer waters, Julia led me below.

It was no time for the sweets of luxury; they would come, in their season, with the swallow and the lime flowers. Now on the rough water there was a formality to be observed, no more. It was as though a deed of conveyance of her narrow loins had been drawn and sealed. I was making my first entry as the freeholder of a property I would enjoy and develop at leisure.

We dined that night high up in the ship, in the restaurant, and saw through the bow windows the stars come out and sweep across the sky as once, I remembered, I had seen them sweep across the towers and gables of Oxford. The stewards promised tomorrow night the band would play again and the place be full. We had better book now, they said, if we wanted a good table.

'Oh dear,' said Julia, 'where can we hide in fair weather, we orphans of the storm?'

Commentary

The beginning of the extract is romantically charged; the sun is personified, and is a moral arbitrator, 'putting the lights to shame'. The sky later possesses a lyrical beauty. Indeed, the elements, the sky, the storm, the sea, the sun and the stars provide a romantic inevitability to the consummation of the passion. Passion is an overwhelming force, not to be resisted. The lovers whirl together as in a storm.

The narrator places his actions in the passive voice, 'I found myself flung across her'. And he makes it clear that Julia is in charge. Julia takes control both at the beginning of the lengthy paragraph, leading him 'up to the boat-deck', and later, through her speech and her actions which parallel the beginning. She initiates the love-making by saying, 'Yes, now' and it is she who leads him below. Yet earlier he mentions his arms which had 'held her prisoner'. Amid the romantic movement of the ship, this is surely an unsettling image of entrapment, and possession; yet syntactically it is part of an extraordinarily lengthy sentence, which focuses on their enforced embrace once on the boat deck. Is it seamless and unbroken in order to mirror the rise and fall of the ship over the ocean? The lexis is still that of romance and passion – note 'wide and golden sky', 'she was thrown forward onto my heart'.

However, the short paragraph beginning 'It was no time for the sweets of luxury' is disquieting. What does this mean? It is abstract and terse. What are the 'sweets of luxury'? 'Swallow' suggests the arrival of the summer, 'lime flowers' the height of summer. 'Julia' has vanished in this paragraph. The syntax is clipped and mechanistic. The narrator is the active subject, 'she' the passive object. But this is the paragraph where intercourse takes place, not the previous paragraph which contains all the apparatus of romance – the ship, the waves, the sunset. Here, the imagery is of property and possession. The language appears to defer meaning too, as the words do not describe what is happening, but project a male sense of ownership upon the female body.

The final paragraph restores the couple to society and blends past (Oxford memories), present (the meal) and future (the band will play tomorrow). From being down 'below' they are now in a position of prominence 'high up'. Julia has a voice. She defines their adulterous isolation in terms of an unanswerable, rhetorical question. 'Where can we hide in fair weather, we orphans of the storm?'

Different critical perspectives

Feminist reading
Where does the balance of power lie? The narrator is male, but Julia is in control at first. She brings Charles on deck, then initiates the return below deck, to make love, but within the paragraph is presented as 'clinging to Charles', passive and surrendering, thrown on to his heart. Here there is a hint that she is his property, she 'clung to me', her 'face still pressed to mine'. As suggested above, she becomes masculine property when they make love. The language of possession becomes more overt, controlling and male. Julia has become 'the other', an anonymous female body. As Virginia Woolf writes on gendered language in *A Room of One's Own,* male novelists write 'a natural prose, swift but not slovenly, expressive but not precious, taking their own tint without ceasing to be common property'. The male 'I' dominates in this paragraph. The syntax is balanced, purposeful and controlled. Feminist critics would interpret this passage as an example of phallocentric discourse.

Marxist approach
A Marxist critic too would examine the balance of power within the text, both between the couple and their position in the liner's hierarchy, the liner as a microcosm of society. The semantic field of property is significant: 'I was making my first entry as the freeholder of the property I would enjoy and develop at leisure.'

Charles' rhetoric is that of a successful capitalist, with time for both business and leisure. The Marxist would be aware too of the fact that the couple enjoy a privileged position on the liner. They walk away from 'the flying smuts of the smoke stack', representative of manual labour and industry. They are treated deferentially by the steward, who nevertheless represents alienation, distancing hierarchically, a feature of Marxist criticism. Oxford too comes into the picture as a given place of privilege, and this is part of the lexis of luxury.

Psychoanalytical approach

The psychoanalytic critic might consider how sexuality is presented in this passage, noting the image of the hand in the pocket as representative of coition, in much the same way as the finger in the glove is used in *The Changeling* by Middleton and Rowley (see Part 2, page 39). What is the symbolic significance of the sea? Does the enforced physicality of their encounter on deck represent, metonymically, the intercourse which is never described? The movement of the ship, the 'dark horizon of tumbling water', the moments of stasis and violent involuntary energy all symbolise the sexual act, the post-coital meal, their communion.

Structuralist approach

The structuralist critic would, as the name suggests, focus upon the structure of the passage. She or he would take note, as we have seen, of the parallels and contrasts within the text. The most basic binary opposite would be the male / female divide, but the structuralist critic would note also, above and below, the deck and the sea, movement and stasis, light and dark, concealment and openness. How does language communicate meaning in and through these lexical binaries? What is the relationship between direct and indirect speech?

Post-structuralism

Terry Eagleton sees post-structuralism as 'knowing the text as it cannot know itself'. Derrida writes that deconstruction 'must always aim at a certain relationship, unperceived by the writer, between what he commands and what he does not command of the patterns of language that he uses'. A post-structuralist critic therefore, would focus on the inconsistencies within this passage. Why is there such an abrupt shift of tone within the text? Why is Julia silenced? Why do his arms hold 'her prisoner'? It is important to understand what the word *aporia* means in criticism. It comes from the Greek for 'abyss', literally a gap, an emptiness where the reader puzzles over meaning. These *aporia* point to the deferral of meaning, emphasising ambiguity.

▶ How many contradictions can you detect in the text?

Narratology

A narratologist would focus on how the story is told. Firstly, how is the story structured? He or she may consider the movement 'down' to make love before rising 'up' to dine aloft. Is the action 'mimetic', as though it is dramatised – we are shown as readers what is occurring – or is it 'diegetic', parcelled up into some kind of summary, an overview? It is possible to distinguish the two different types of narrative within the text. The lovemaking is presented diegetically, whereas the time on deck is mimetic. Both means of discourse are therefore used within the text. The narratologist is interested also in the structures or architecture of time and space.

What is the place of the narrator within the story? *Brideshead Revisited* is narrated throughout from the point of view of Charles Ryder, one of the main characters in the story, a 'homodiegetic' narrator, as the theorist Gerard Genette writes 'present as a character in the story he tells'. If he were to observe from the margins, he would be a 'heterodiegetic' narrator, such as Mr Lockwood in *Wuthering Heights*.

Other contextual influences: the novel and the author

Placing this extract within the context of the novel itself opens up possibilities of further critical interpretation. Brideshead, the magnificent home of the Marchmain family, has enormous emotional pulling power within the novel. At this stage, Charles' sense of nostalgia for what is lost – his golden sybaritic youth at Oxford when he first encountered Sebastian and his consequent visits to Brideshead, where he was welcomed as part of the family – is overwhelming. Therefore the imagery of conveyancing, taking possession of, and entering a house, resonates with meaning. Is the author suggesting that Charles would like to be the next Lord Marchmain? Or, could it be that he is sublimating / transferring his desires, and he actually longs to make love to Julia's lost brother, Sebastian?

The novel's subtitle, *The sacred and profane memories of Captain Charles Ryder,* provides the information that Charles is in the army, and indeed the whole story is narrated retrospectively from the Second World War, a time of austerity. Thus, the phrase 'the sweets of luxury' focuses the reader on a lost and golden past, possibly never to be recovered. From the word 'sacred' we understand that religion is to play a part in the novel. The Marchmains are Catholic aristocracy, and therefore the whole text may be read in theological terms. Do you consider that the *descent* to the cabin to make love has any theological significance? 'Profane' may mean secular – it may also mean blasphemous and obscene. Are the lovers, through their adulterous liaison, consigning themselves to Hell as Paolo and Francesca did in Canto 5 of Dante's *Inferno* many centuries before?

The 1959 Preface gives Waugh's retrospective view of the text: 'Its theme – the operation of divine grace on a group of diverse but closely connected characters'. Does it help our understanding of the text to learn that Waugh was a Catholic convert, received into the church in 1930, the year after he divorced his wife?

Revisions

Waugh himself was unhappy about some of the more sentimental, baroque and florid passages. He revised the text in 1959, excising and rewriting passages. In particular, the passage which caused him most anxiety was the one quoted above. In his diary of 9th May 1944 he wrote:

> I feel very much the futility of describing sexual emotions without describing the sexual act; I should like to give as much detail as I have of the meals, to the two coitions – with his wife and Julia. It would be no more or less obscene than to leave them to the reader's imagination, which in this case cannot be as acute as mine. There is a gap in which the reader will insert his own sexual habits instead of those of my characters.

Waugh highlights the *aporia,* the gaps, which are such a feature of post-structuralist criticism. Why does he feel that he is not able to describe the sexual act? Note that he links 'meals' with 'the act of coition'. In his reflections, he does not envisage his readers making intertextual links to lovemaking they may have read about, but instead imagines his reader calling upon his or her own experience. Does this say something about the nature of erotic writing in the 1940s? To what extent is the sexual act masked by metaphor and allusion?

▶ The extract on pages 97–98 is the revised 1959 version. Here is what Waugh originally wrote, in 1944. Compare the two versions, using whatever critical approaches seem to you to be most appropriate.

> Now on the rough water I was made free of her narrow loins and, it seemed now, assuaging that fierce appetite, cast a burden which I had borne all my life, toiled under, not knowing its nature – now, while the waves still broke and thundered on the prow, the act of possession was a symbol, a rite of ancient origin and solemn meaning.

Reading D.H Lawrence

D.H. Lawrence (1885–1930) was one of the most boldly experimental and innovative writers on sexuality in the 20th century. His work has been admired, disparaged, censored, parodied and ignored in equal measure. Here is a range of critical writing on Lawrence.

Stephen Potter *D.H. Lawrence: a First Study*

This very first 'study' of Lawrence's work was published in 1930. In the introduction the author sets out his intentions as follows: 'Lawrence died on the 3rd of March 1930, when these pages were in proof. Although what I have written deals largely with the autobiographical side of his work, the book is not a biography but a comment on certain aspects of his writings.' Potter considers Lawrence's readership, and possibly by implication the target audience of his own book, as 'youngish, normally educated, somewhat conventional men'. The introduction makes further questionable assertions:

1   For every one person who reads his books there are ten who understand that what he writes has generally something to do with *sex,* that he speaks often of the *unconscious,* that he uses the word *dark* as often as Dante uses the word *light,* and that he believes in the importance of savages, animals and the Holy Ghost.
2   He hates ideas – 'like nails stuck in the bark of a growing tree'.

But in Potter's commentary upon Lawrence's work it is possible to detect the kernel of various critical approaches which are current today. He states that Lawrence is a writer with a philosophy and makes reference to the good horse / bad horse analogy in Phaedrus / Plato (see Part 1, page 10). He argues that Lawrence reverses Plato and embraces the dark. Note the implied reference to binary opposition here, a feature of structuralism: 'The novelty of this reversed idealism, and the fact that Lawrence propounds it in most of his books has its advantages. His method of stating every question in terms of the opposition of two contraries has force.'

With regard to Lawrence's poems and his relationship with Frieda, his wife, Potter employs the lexis of psychoanalysis: 'There is also the struggle of the wish, put down in brief poems, to melt away the ego barrier, the hard personality part which is a fence between each of them. This is achieved: Lawrence's great wish is granted: the mounting wave in him bursts in action.'

However, a simply Freudian reading of his novels is firmly dismissed later. In responding to the question as to whether Lawrence is the novelist of psychoanalysis, Potter states:

But though Lawrence sometimes uses its terminology, the point of his books will be missed if they are interpreted on the pathological basis of a science which puts 'infantile experience' in the position of the Fates and Furies of classical tragedy and makes it, with its power of deciding events before they have happened, as fatal to dramatic interest as any *deus ex machina.* Power over their own fates, or perhaps power to abandon themselves to their fates, is an essential implication behind the life of his characters.

Potter champions Lawrence's take on sex, by writing vehemently about what Lawrence hated. Both critic and subject unite in their condemnation of the debasement of sex in the material world. The list includes: misogyny, 'sex an amusing weakness', 'those who write clearly, calmly and nicely about it,' psychoanalysis – because 'sex is the only motive' – and co-education because 'the nice clean intimacy which we now so admire between the sexes is sterilising. It makes neuters. Later on, no deep, magical sex-life is possible.' But how does Lawrence narrate sex? Potter's conclusions are remarkably prescient: 'Coition itself he describes again and again – never generalising, each time taking a different kind of pairing and showing the different experience possible in each.'

Writing seventy years later, in 'Narrating Sexuality: The Rainbow' in *The Cambridge Companion to D.H. Lawrence*, Marianna Torgovnick also stresses how Lawrence narrates sexuality, with 'innovation and courage':

> He is keenly aware that each encounter between two people can have a very different emotional surround which is sometimes consistent with earlier encounters and sometimes not. …
>
> He asserts a spiritual dimension to sexuality: sex in all of these texts gives access to a sense of the eternal.

Like Potter, she concludes that Lawrence's writing transcends the pornography of his time through its courageous experimentation and willingness to *narrate*: 'Lawrence investigated sex not just as mechanical, physical action, but as a tissue of thoughts, fantasies and emotions. Lawrence *narrated* sex. Few others have even tried.'

Anais Nin *D.H. Lawrence: An Unprofessional Study*

How did contemporary women respond to D.H. Lawrence? Anais Nin (1903–1977) earned her living as a writer of stories, essays and erotica. Tellingly, this monograph on Lawrence was published privately, in 1932. She also anticipates Torgovnik by focusing on how Lawrence narrates sex. She quotes Lawrence on the subject: 'And don't, with the nasty prying mind, drag it (sex) out from its deeps and finger it and force it, and shatter the rhythm it keeps when it's left alone, as it stirs and rouses and sleeps.' The following quotation is significant:

> Lawrence's descriptions of the undercurrents of body and mind were but means of bringing to the surface many feelings that we do not sincerely acknowledge in ourselves. Freud and Jung have done this but they are essentially scientists and are read with the detachment and objectivity of scientific research. Lawrence's characters, whether in poetry, allegory, or prophecy, are actors who speak with the very accents of our emotions; and before we are aware, our feelings

become identified and involved with theirs. Some have recoiled from such an awakening, often unpleasant; many have dreaded having to acknowledge his power over their physical sensations, as well as to face in plain words, the real meaning of their fantasies.

Like Potter, Nin acknowledges the work of Freud, but dismisses him as a 'scientist'. The real focus here is on Lawrence's language. Nin's most quoted remark is that Lawrence 'had a complete realisation of the feelings of women. In fact, very often he wrote *as a woman* would write.' She praises him for his empathy, citing particularly his sensitivity in *Lady Chatterley's Lover*, where 'every moment of the relationship reveals the woman's feelings as well as the man's, and the woman's with the most delicate and subtle acuteness'. She develops her argument with the assertion that 'his suspicion of the intellect is of course, close to the feminine nature. He confides in the intuition. He battles for the clairvoyance of it, through many chaotic pages. And this is purely a feminine battle. His moments of *blind* reactions strike a response in women. It is the first time that a man has so wholly and completely expressed woman accurately.'

▶ How far do you agree? Are men ever capable of 'expressing' women, of 'writing' women accurately? How would a feminist critic interpret the extracts from *The Rainbow* (Part 3, page 89)?

Nin defines Lawrence's linguistic experimentalism in terms of the arts: his prose has 'the bulgingness of sculpture, the nuance of paint, the rhythm of movement, of dancing, sound, musicality, cadence'. When she sums up her thoughts on how Lawrence 'writes' sexuality, Nin's own lexis is initially sexual – 'penetration', 'deep reaching', 'channels' – but concludes with the simile of Lawrence as painter, focusing the reader's attention on the body as artefact.

> His sensorial penetration is complete. That is why his most abstract thought is always deep reaching: it is really concrete, it passes through the channels of the senses. Writing as a rule is characterised by either one quality or another. The intellectual dressing of abstractions is a familiar weakness of writers. But Lawrence worked like a painter who works on the anatomy, from which he paints the figure and over that the draperies.

Reading Toni Morrison's *Beloved*

Lawrence has been praised for writing as a woman would write. The critic Hélène Cixous, in her essay 'The Laugh of the Medusa' (1981), suggests that if male discourse is grammatical and logical, there should be a way of writing that is free from these restrictions. She links it to female physiology, the body.

Women must write through their bodies, they must invent the impregnable language that will wreck partitions, classes, and rhetorics, regulations and codes, they must submerge, cut through ... such is the strength of women that, sweeping away syntax, breaking that famous thread, (just a tiny little thread, they say) which acts for men as a surrogate umbilical cord...

Tony Morrison's groundbreaking novel, *Beloved,* (1987) is based on the true story of the slave mother, Margaret Garner, who killed her child when the slave hunters came to catch them. When questioned, she replied that 'she was unwilling to have her children suffer as she had done'. And the body dominates the narrative: the slave mother of the novel, Sethe, is tortured and beaten, milked like a cow, gives birth. She murders her 'crawling already' baby to put her in another place, away from the slave catchers. The dead child seemingly returns in the mysterious body of Beloved, a body which grows and swells as Sethe's diminishes. Baby Suggs, the grandmother of Sethe's children, preaches a sermon on the holiness of the slave body:

Here, in this here place, we flesh; flesh that weeps, laughs; flesh that dances in bare feet on grass. Love it. Love it hard. Yonder they do not love your flesh. They despise it. They don't love your eyes; they just as soon pick 'em out. No more do they love the skin on your back. Yonder they flay it.

Margaret Atwood, in reviewing Toni Morrison's *Beloved,* echoes Cixous. She enthuses that 'her versatility and technical and emotional range appear to know no bounds'. Morrison herself, interviewed about the 'richness' of her work, had this to say:

They always say my writing is rich. It's not – what's rich, if there is any richness, is what the reader gets and brings him or herself. That's part of the way in which the tale is told. The folk tales are told in such a way that whoever is listening is in it and can shape it and figure it out. It's not over because it stops. It lingers and it's passed on. It's passed on and someone else can alter it later ... One of the things that's important to me is the powerful imaginative way in which we deconstructed and reconstructed reality in order to get through.

('In the Realm of Responsibility: A Conversation with
Toni Morrison', 1988)

And on slavery:

From a woman's point of view, in terms of confronting the problems of where the world is now, black women had to deal with 'post-modern' problems in the nineteenth century and earlier. These things had to be addressed by black people a long time ago. Certain kinds of dissolution, the loss of and the need to reconstruct certain kinds of stability. Certain kinds of madness, deliberately going mad in order, as one of the characters says in the book, 'not to lose your mind'.

('Living Memory: A meeting with Toni Morrison', 1993)

The psychoanalytical critic Peter Nicholls, in the essay 'The Belated Postmodern: History, Phantoms, and Toni Morrison' (1992), reads the figure of Beloved as follows:

Who is Beloved? A revenant, someone who comes back, she seems to offer precisely what we have always yearned for, the past made good, an origin restored, 'my girl come home' ... But she is not that; or at least she is always more than that, at once Sethe's daughter and an African lost in the Middle Passage – and even as Sethe's daughter, she is not what she was, but grown to the age she would have been, her neck bearing 'the little curved shadow' left by the handsaw. This play of contradiction seems now the very mark of the Postmodern, issuing in an insistence that something (someone) can be two things at once, that two things can occupy the same space, that the origin is irreducibly doubled.

He also interprets Beloved psychoanalytically as 'a figure of thwarted love, of the body literally possessed by others. Her belated appearance is traumatic in Freud's sense precisely because it embodies an overwhelming desire, a now unrepresentable excess of the emotional need suppressed under slavery "to love any thing that much was dangerous"' (*Icon Readers' Guide: Toni Morrison Beloved*).

▶ Consider the following extract in the light of critical approaches cited. How does Morrison invent a new discourse? What is the effect of 'sweeping away syntax'?

I am Beloved and she is mine   I see her take flowers away from leaves she puts them in a round basket   the leaves are not for her   she fills the basket   she opens the grass   I would help her but the clouds are in the way   how can I say the things that are pictures   I am not separate from her   there is no place where I stop   her face is my own and I want to be there in the place where her face is and looking at it too   a hot thing.

5 | How to write about the literature of love

- What sort of text am I writing about?

- How do structure, form and language shape meaning?

- What useful comparisons and connections can I make with other texts?

- What can I say about the context in which this text was written and which it has been received?

- How can I usefully refer to the views of other readers and critics?

When writing on the topic of the literature of love, you will have the opportunity to display a variety of literary skills. Close critical analysis should be at the heart of all your reading, and should inform everything that you write. For example:

- You may be required to compare two texts of the same genre, while making valid connections and links with your wider reading in the same genre. For instance, you may be asked to compare two sonnets, from different literary periods, on the theme of betrayal in love. An understanding of the development of the love sonnet through time is important, but it would be perfectly acceptable to refer to any poetry on the theme of betrayal from your wider reading.

- You may also make comparisons across genres, as well as within genres. Again, you could be asked to compare an extract from a play, such as the last scene of Harold Pinter's *Betrayal*, with an extract from a post-1990 novel, such as *Atonement* by Ian McEwan. Of course, it is possible that your prose text could be non-fiction, such as a love letter concealing a betrayal or an extract from a column in a magazine giving advice on coping with a partner's infidelity.

- You may be asked to write an extended essay on a topic related to the literature of love. Obviously, your texts will be linked thematically, and you will probably refer to the three different genres; poetry, prose and drama. Alternatively, your essay might compare the treatment of love in the novels of, say, Jane Austen and E.M. Forster or in the poetry of Elizabeth Barrett Browning and Carol Ann Duffy.

Part 5 begins with a close critical comparison of two short lyrics on the theme of desire, to be followed by two extracts from novels on 'desire attained' – the kiss.

Finally, there is a discussion of ways to examine connections between a poem, the end of a short story and an extract from a Shakespeare play, all linked by the theme of love and memory.

Comparing poems

A comparison of the anonymous 15th-century lyric 'Western Wind' with 'Wild nights', written by Emily Dickinson in the mid-19th century, illustrates how two writers, separated by time, possibly gender, and culture, write about desire: To begin with 'Western Wind':

> Western wind, when will thou blow
> The small rain down can rain?
> Christ, if my love were in my arms
> And I in my bed again!

This is one of the shortest, earliest and most self-contained love lyrics you will ever encounter. The speaker conveys a desire to embrace the beloved: note how, structurally, this desire lies centrally enfolded in the poem on the third line. The first line is an apostrophe, addressing the personified Western wind directly; the third and fourth lines yearn for an imagined state of future bliss.

The simplicity of the language is striking. Every word, apart from the first and last, is a monosyllable. Do you consider that this makes the emotion seem more heartfelt, more elemental? Does it foreground particular words, which may otherwise appear unimportant, such as the preposition 'in'? Does the assonance in the second line reflect the pattering down of the rain? What contrasts occur within the poem?

The poem does raise literary questions, some of which may seem at first unanswerable but may become self evident after reading the second poem:

- What is the function of the elements within the poem?

- Why does the third line begin with the word 'Christ'? What is its effect?

Before even beginning to study 'Wild nights' in detail, there are some contextual factors worth noting. It was written by the 19th-century American poet, Emily Dickinson, who craved poetic anonymity during her lifetime. Very few of her one thousand, seven hundred and eighty-nine untitled poems were published while she was alive. Should this poem therefore be titled? Whose title is it? What is the relationship between the speaker and the text? Is the speaker Emily Dickinson herself? 'Wild nights' appears to adopt a lyric format similar to 'Western Wind', extended for three stanzas:

> Wild nights – Wild nights!
> Were I with thee

Wild nights should be
Our luxury!

Futile – the winds –
To a Heart in port –
Done with the Compass –
Done with the Chart!

Rowing in Eden –
Ah! the Sea!
Might I but moor – tonight –
In thee!

The typography of the poem is startling at first glance. Emily Dickinson makes erratic use of capital letters for nouns. Dashes replace conventional punctuation, except for the exclamation marks. It appears at first reading that the 'Wild nights' are apostrophised, like 'Western Wind', but is this the case? The capitalisation, the exclamation mark and the assonance within 'wild' and 'night' make the phrase an incantatory cry of anticipated sexual pleasure. The desired beloved is directly addressed as 'thee', which thus supplies the triple rhyme 'thee,' 'be' – climaxing in 'luxury', the only non-monosyllabic word in the first stanza. Is 'luxury' lingeringly drawn out, to mirror the endless night of ecstasy? But, as in 'Western Wind', the imagined bliss is dependent upon the conditionals, here 'were', 'should', 'if': a state of joy not yet arrived at. If it were to occur, 'I' and 'thee' would become 'our'.

The language is clearly metaphorical in the second stanza. 'Port', 'Compass' and 'Chart' suggest navigation, but the journey is complete. The syntactic parallelism, the anaphora ('Done with the…') and, again, the exclamation, imply triumphant arrival. The heart has found its home, its safe harbour. There may be a religious connection with the words of St Augustine, who writes: 'Our hearts are restless till we find our rest in Thee.' In the literature of love, note how often the sea is used as a metaphor for passion.

How does the third stanza conclude the poem? Can it be compared with the end of 'Western Wind'? Be aware of ellipsis, or things unsaid: who is 'Rowing in Eden'? What is the effect of the participle, 'Rowing'? Why 'Eden'? Are there echoes of other literary texts here? The participle suggests a continuous present, an existence in a Paradise gained, an Eden, but is this a wish, or a statement of fact? (The poem 'Bermudas' by the metaphysical poet Andrew Marvell, uses the same conceit.) Again, note that the conditional is used, and emphasised, through the alliteration of 'might' and 'moor'.

Look at the verbal coupling in the poem, which is used to convey the idea of rowing tightly and vigorously, for example, the repeated 'Done', the internal rhyme of 'might' and 'tonight', the alliteration of 'might' and 'moor', with the repeated 'm' sounds, and the repeated 'e' rhyming, climaxing in 'Sea' and thee'. Does this coupling suggest that 'rowing' is a metaphor for making love? Certainly, both poems end with the wish to be enfolded in the arms of a lover – 'Western Wind' *after* the wind, and the gentle rain, which may, metonymically or symbolically, represent passion / sex.

Finally, be aware of the religious references in both poems. The speaker in 'Wild nights' hopes to reach paradise, a spiritual nirvana, by 'Rowing in Eden'. The exclamation 'Christ' in the first poem may suggest a desire to be at one with Christ. Is this sacred or profane?

To sum up: both poems show the reader something of the nature of desire, attainable and yet ever unattainable, the ecstasy forever held at bay (or suspended) by the conditionals 'if', 'were' and 'might'.

▶ How far has reading one of these poems in the context of the other helped to sharpen your response to each lyric?

Responding to prose

If you are asked to compare two prose passages, these are likely to be extracts from longer works; thus it is helpful to have some understanding of the contexts from which they are taken.

- You may want to consider at what stage each extract occurs in the novel or short story and whether they appear to be from the same historical / literary period.

- From whose point of view is each passage narrated? For instance is the narrator omniscient and intrusive, or do the events unfold from the point of view of one of the characters? Do your sympathies shift as you read and how has the writer brought this about?

- What is the structure of each passage? Is there a significant climax or epiphany in each one? Do the writers use any similar lexical or syntactic features?

- It is useful to remind yourself why the two passages have been selected. The features they have in common should helpfully illuminate the differences.

The following two extracts are taken from *The Portrait of a Lady* (1881) by Henry James, and *A Room with a View* by E.M. Forster (1908). Read each through carefully. Which do you consider to be the more romantic?

This extract occurs near the end of *The Portrait of a Lady*. Casper Goodwood, a former suitor, is urging Isabel to escape from a loveless and confining marriage. 'You're the most unhappy of women, and your husband's the deadliest of fiends.'

The rest was that she had never been loved before. She believed it, but this was different; this was the hot wind of the desert, at the approach of which the others dropped dead, like the mere sweet airs of the garden. It wrapped her about; it lifted her off her feet, while the very taste of it, as of something potent, acrid and strange, forced open her set teeth …

Isabel gave a long murmur, like a creature in pain: it was as if he was pressing something that hurt her. 'The world's very small,' she said at random; she had an intense desire to appear to resist. She said it at random, to hear herself say something; but it was not what she meant. The world in truth, had never seemed so large; it seemed to open out, all round her, to take the form of a mighty sea, where she floated in fathomless waters. She had wanted help, and here was help; it had come in a rushing torrent. I know not whether she believed everything he said; but she believed just then that to let him take her in his arms would be the next best thing to her dying. This belief, for a moment, was a kind of rapture, in which she felt herself sink and sink. In the movement she seemed to beat with her feet, in order to catch herself, to feel something to rest on. …

She clasped her hands: her eyes were streaming with tears.
   'As you love me, as you pity me, leave me alone!'
   He glared at her a moment through the dusk, and the next instant she felt his arms around her and his lips on her own lips. His kiss was like white lightning, a flash that spread, and spread again, and stayed: and it was extraordinarily as if, while she took it, she felt each thing in his hard manhood that had least pleased her, each aggressive fact of his face, his figure, his presence, justified of its intense identity and made one with this act of possession. So had she heard of those wrecked and under water following a train of images before they sink. But when darkness returned she was free.

In this extract from *A Room with a View*, Cecil Vyse has proposed, successfully, to Lucy Honeychurch, but, as yet, has not kissed her. Here, he points out the omission.

   'Lucy, I want to ask something of you that I have never asked before.'
At the serious note in his voice she stepped frankly and kindly towards him.
   'What Cecil?'
   'Hitherto never – not even that day on the lawn when you agreed to marry me –'

He became self-conscious and kept glancing round to see if they were observed. His courage had gone.

'Yes?'

'Up to now I have never kissed you.' She was as scarlet as if he had put the whole thing most indelicately.

'No – more you have,' she stammered.

'Then I ask you – may I now?'

'Of course you may, Cecil. You might before. I won't run at you, you know.'

At that supreme moment he was conscious of nothing but absurdities. Her reply was inadequate. She gave such a business-like lift to her veil. As he approached her he found time to wish that he could recoil. As he touched her, his gold pince-nez became dislodged and flattened between them.

Such was the embrace. He considered, with truth, that it had been a failure. Passion should believe itself irresistible. It should forget civility and consideration and all the other curses of a refined nature. Above all, it should never ask for leave where there is a right of way. Why could he not do as any labourer or navvy – nay, as any young man behind the counter would have done? He recast the scene. Lucy was standing flower-like by the water; he rushed up and took her in his arms; she rebuked him, permitted him, and revered him ever after for his manliness. For he believed that women revere men for their manliness.

They left the pool in silence …

The kiss is central to both passages – the James' passage framed theatrically by Casper's hyperbolic words 'your husband's the deadliest of fiends', and the author's statement 'she had never been loved before'. Social convention dictates the second kiss, to cement the engagement between Lucy and Cecil.

What are each author's narrative methods? Henry James appears to narrate the events from Isabel's point of view, although the presence of the author looms behind her. The narrative stance in the second extract is less easy to discern. As David Lodge writes in *The Art of Fiction* (1992) 'Modern fiction has tended to suppress or eliminate the authorial voice, by presenting the action through the consciousness of the characters, or by handing over to them the narrative task itself.' Do you think that each author appears to retreat as the extract progresses? Why is this?

Who controls the events in each extract? It is easy to say that the men appear to be in charge. Goodwood initiates the kissing, as does Cecil, but the roles that Isabel and Lucy adopt are interesting. How much resistance, passive or otherwise, is written into the script?

To begin to answer this question you may find it helpful to compare the place of speech in each extract. The Forster passage reads like a modern comedy of manners; indeed Cecil is painfully aware of himself as a public persona upon the matrimonial stage – he is 'the fiancé'. His awkwardness is conveyed through his hesitations, formalised pomposity ('Hitherto') and qualifications. The three times repeated 'never' gives his words a kind of doomed impotence, let alone his articulation of the very word 'kiss' which causes Lucy physical embarrassment: she blushes as she registers her discomfort. Her clipped, tripartite response seals Cecil's fate. Note how she unconsciously parodies his asking permission by playing with the word 'may': 'Of course you may, Cecil. You might before. I won't run at you, you know.'

You may think that the speech in the first extract has nothing in common with the extract from *A Room with a View*. It seems as though most of the writing is Isabel's deeply felt interior monologue, thus any speech at all is superfluous. And yet a significant connection can be made. We have seen above how Lucy apparently gives Cecil verbal permission to kiss. Here are Isabel's words to Goodwood at the same stage:

> She clasped her hands: her eyes were streaming with tears.
> 'As you love me, as you pity me, leave me alone!'

Surely these are words of rejection. She is pushing Casper away. Like Lucy, her speech is in three sections, the rhythmic anaphora driving the climax. The only other words she has previously uttered have been 'The world is very small.' But the authorial voice directs the reader to understand that this was not what she meant – that in fact her spoken word was incapable of communicating her true emotion. Therefore, neither Lucy's words nor Isabel's are to be taken at face value. Lucy's words granting permission are the kiss of death to Cecil, whereas the intense poeticism of Isabel's utterance is the inevitable precursor to the kiss.

The kiss in *A Room with a View* comes as an anti-climax. The sentences are short and jarring: the 'supreme' moment, laden with such high social expectation, is surreal, distasteful and clumsy. What do the squashed 'pince-nez' represent symbolically? The kiss is experienced completely from the point of view of Cecil, and although there has been previously both blushing and awkwardness between them, his response is cerebral, a sort of calculated intellectual evaluation of a procedure which has failed.

▶ To what extent do Cecil's musings in the final paragraph from the extract from *A Room with a View* provide a helpful commentary on the kiss between Isabel and Casper in *The Portrait of a Lady*? Does the writer allow the reader to feel any sympathy for him?

Cecil, as if he were a film director (though the novel predates the era of cinema), reshoots the dismal scene in his mind to give it a truly romantic tinge. Desperate to erase the memory of failure, he recasts himself as the ultimate romantic, Byronic hero – a Casper Goodwood in fact, taking the protesting maiden by force and subduing her will to his. But this is the very task that James has set himself – to describe an epiphanic moment in Isabel's life, where she comes emotionally and sexually alive.

▶ Is James here presenting a male view of a sort of ultimate female fantasy? How is it done?

First, consider how James uses extended metaphorical writing to convey the way that Casper overpowers Isabel. Is there any ambivalence in the metaphor of the 'hot wind of the desert'? Might this in fact suggest that any awakening to love is in fact doomed and barren? How is the sea / drowning imagery developed? What does this suggest about the relationship between life and death? Is she drowning in passion, or brought to a new life?

You should also be aware of the effect of James' extended periodic sentences. How is the very moment of the kiss actually described? Forster creates a gap (the end of one paragraph and the beginning of another) to indicate that the kiss was a failure, whereas James' sentence is the longest in the whole passage and it is notable that the imagery changes to 'white lightning' – an image echoing *Romeo and Juliet*. Again there is the sense of impossibility which has been such a feature of the whole passage. How can lightning stay and stay? How can something as ephemeral as a kiss be given permanence? Is James suggesting that her resistance is no resistance at all?

▶ How does the James passage compare with other moments of passion in the literature of love? Look at the extracts from *Wuthering Heights and Brideshead Revisited* (Part 3, page 87 and Part 4, page 97).

▶ How might a critic writing from a Marxist perspective interpret the imagery of possession in the first extract and the references to 'labourers and navvies' in the second?

▶ Both passages were written by men. How might a feminist critic read them? Is it significant that there is no mention of Casper's emotions and feelings throughout, apart from his 'hard manhood'?

Comparing across genres

The following three texts are all connected thematically. The first extract is taken from the end of Shakespeare's play *Antony and Cleopatra* (1606). Antony has just died at his own hand. Dolabella, one of Caesar's followers, visits the imprisoned Cleopatra. She speaks to him of her dead lover:

CLEOPATRA: I dreamt there was an emperor, Antony.
                    O, such another sleep, that I might see
                    But such another man!
DOLABELLA: If it might please ye –
CLEOPATRA::   His face was as the heav'ns, and therein stuck
                    A sun and moon, which kept their course and lighted
                    The little O, the earth.
DOLABELLA: Most sovereign creature –
CLEOPATRA::   His legs bestrid the ocean; his reared arm
                    Crested the world; his voice was propertied
                    As all the tuned spheres, and that to friends;
                    But when he meant to quail and shake the orb,
                    He was as rattling thunder. For his bounty,
                    There was no winter in't; an autumn 'twas
                    That grew the more by reaping. His delights
                    Were dolphin-like; they showed his back above
                    The elements they lived in. In his livery
                    Walked crowns and crownets; realms and islands were
                    As plates dropped from his pocket.
DOLABELLA: Cleopatra –
CLEOPATRA::   Think you there was or might be such a man
                    As this I dreamt of?
DOLABELLA: Gentle madam, no.
CLEOPATRA::   You lie up to the hearing of the gods.
                    But if there be nor ever were one such,
                    It's past the size of dreaming. Nature wants stuff
                    To vie strange forms with fancy; yet t'imagine
                    An Antony were Nature's piece 'gainst fancy,
                    Condemning shadows quite.   (V.ii.76–99)

The sonnet 'Remember' by Christina Rossetti was published in 1862:

Remember me when I am gone away,
Gone far away into the silent land,
When you can no more hold me by the hand,
Nor I half turn to go yet turning stay.
Remember me when no more day by day
You tell me of our future that you planned:
Only remember me; you understand
It will be late to counsel then or pray.
Yet if you should forget me for a while

And afterwards remember, do not grieve:
For if the darkness and corruption leave
A vestige of the thoughts that once I had,
Better by far you should forget and smile
Than that you should remember and be sad.

The prose extract is taken from the conclusion to the short story 'Remember This Moment, Remember Us', from his collection of short stories, *The Body* (2002), by Hanif Kureishi. Anna and Rick decide to tape a video message for their two-year-old son, Daniel, to be watched when he is Rick's age – 45:

Although they haven't decided what to say, they will go ahead with the filming certain that something will occur to them. This spontaneity may make their little dispatch to the future seem less portentous.

Rick lugs the Christmas tree over towards the sofa where they will sit for the message and turns on the lights. He regards his wife through the camera. She has let down her hair.

'How splendid you look!'

She asks, 'Should I take my slippers off?'

'Anna, your fluffies won't be immortalised. I'll frame it down to our waists.'

She gets up and looks at him through the eye piece, telling him he's as fine as he'll ever be. He switches on the camera and notices there is only about fifteen minutes of tape left.

With the camera running, he hurries towards the sofa, being careful not to trip up. They will not be able to do this twice. Noticing a half-eaten sardine on the arm of the sofa, he drops it into his pocket.

Rick sits down knowing this will be a sombre business, for he has been, in a sense, already dead for a while. Daniel's idea of him will have been developing for a long while. The two of then will have fallen out on numerous occasions; Daniel might love him but will have disliked him, too, in the normal way. Daniel could hardly have anything but a complicated idea of his past, but these words from eternity will serve as a simple reminder. After all, it is the unloved who are the most dangerous people on earth.

The light on the top of the camera is flashing. As Anna and Rick turn their heads and look into the dark moon of the lens, neither of them speaks for what seems a long time. At last, Rick says, 'Hello there,' rather self-consciously, as though meeting a stranger for the first time. On stage he is never anxious like this. Anna, also at a loss, copies him.

'Hello, Daniel, my son,' she says. 'It's your mummy.'

'And daddy,' Rick says.

'Yes,' she says. 'Here we are!'

'Your parents,' he says.' Remember us? Do you remember this day?' There is a silence; they wonder what to do.

Anna turns to Rick then, placing her hands on his face. She strokes his face as if painting it for the camera. She takes his hand and puts it to her fingers and cheeks. Rick leans over and takes her head between his hands and kisses her on the cheek and on the forehead and on the lips, and she caresses his hair and pulls him to her.

With their heads together, they begin to call out, 'Hello, Dan, we hope you're ok, we just wanted to say hello.'

'Yes, that's right,' chips in the other. 'Hello!'

'We hope you had a good forty-fifth birthday, Dan, with plenty of presents.'

'Yes, and we hope you're well, and your wife, or whoever is it is you're with.'

'Yes, hello there … wife of Dan.'

'And children of Dan,' she adds.

'Yes', he says. 'Children of Dan – however many of you there are, boys or girls or whatever – all the best! A good life to every single one of you!'

'Yes, yes!' she says. 'All of that and more!'

'More, more, more!' Rick says.

After the kissing and stroking and cuddling and saying hello, and with a little time left, they are at a loss as to what to do, but right on cue Dan has an idea. He clambers up from the floor and settles himself on both of them, and they kiss him and pass him between them and get him to wave at himself. When he has done this, he closes his eyes, his head falls into the crook of his mother's arm, and he smacks his lips; and as the tape whirls towards its end, and the rain falls outside and time passes, they want him to be sure of at least this one thing, more than forty years from now, when he looks at these old-fashioned people in the past sitting on the sofa next to the Christmas tree, that on this night they loved him, and they loved each other.

'Goodbye, Daniel,' says Anna.

'Goodbye,' says Rick.

'Goodbye, goodbye,' they say together.

A typical question could ask you to compare the ways in which Shakespeare, Rossetti and Kureishi explore the relationship between love and memory. You will need to refer closely to the writers' choices of form, structure and language, as well as broadening out your work by including appropriate reference to your wider reading.

Thematically, what does each passage have in common? Working backwards, the Kureishi passage depicts a couple creating a postcard though time for their young son, through the means of modern technology, the video; the speaker in the Rossetti poem offers future consolation for the bereaved beyond the grave; and Cleopatra eulogises her beloved departed Antony through the power of her rhetoric.

Already it is possible to differentiate different aspects of love here. Both the Kureishi and the Shakespeare extracts immortalise love, by means of a conscious focus on the mortal body; indeed, it is important to remember here that Kureishi's collection of short stories is entitled *The Body*. The lovers in this story kiss and fondle each other for the camera, as if creating a kind of artefact – 'She stroked his face as if painting it for the camera', a representation of themselves, written on and about the body. Thus their physical bodies are made immortal through the video, and they are bodies in action, kissing, cuddling, and finally tenderly embracing their young son.

Cleopatra too creates a visual image of her Antony, but on a grand, cosmic scale: 'His legs bestrid the ocean; his reared arm / Crested the world.' Her depiction of Antony is god-like and heraldic; in her imagination he transcends mere mortal man, and through her language she consciously creates a memorial of him to arouse both wonder and compassion in her audience. The body is used very differently in 'Remember'. Only 'the hand' is referenced in the Rossetti poem, as a poignant symbol of ultimate separation.

The Kureishi story draws together both love between man and woman, romantic love and love between parent and child. Note how the language used affects this. After the self-conscious adjustment of register – should they speak to him as their little boy or, through imaginative projection, address him as a contemporary? – it settles down into a rhythm of benediction. Simple words, which a two-year old would understand are repeated to shower blessings and messages of good will on the future. 'Yes' drives the speech, and it is worth mentioning that James Joyce concluded *Ulysses* with the words 'and yes I said yes I will yes'.

What connections can be made with the Rossetti sonnet? The title of the sonnet 'Remember' ghosts the Kureishi story, but whereas the couple appear to be making an upbeat video for their son, at a specific time, Christmas, to be watched on a specific date and time (when he is 45), this sonnet is misty and unspecific. The first four lines repay close critical analysis.

The first two words are an imperative – 'Remember me' – and they beg the question 'when?'. The poet states 'when I am gone away', and this is echoed as the line fades into the metaphor of 'the silent land'. What and where is this? Is it, as Hamlet imagines, 'the bourn from which no traveller returns' – death? It is apparently the only image in the whole sonnet. How can a land be silent? Note the ambivalence, or paradox here – that, in fact, the poet creates a memorial to herself beyond the grave, through her speaking voice, which is not 'silent'. Like the legend of Orpheus and Eurydice, her lover will lose her as she enters the 'silent land' forever, so thus the sonnet must earnestly seek to provide consolation.

Further points of comparison are linked to questions of form, grammar and structure.

- How does your wider reading of the love sonnet feed into your reading of 'Remember'? Does this poem have anything in common with early Petrarchan sonnets, or could you compare it to Shakespeare's desire to make the 'fair youth' of the sonnets immortal through his poems? Would it be more appropriate to relate it to the poetry of Elizabeth Barrett Browning? Do you notice any similar linguistic features? Does your reading of the love sonnet suggest to you that in fact this is unconsciously self-centred writing, focused on 'me'?

- Could you make any reference to the endings of modern short stories on the theme of love? What features of the short story can you identify here? An excellent source of modern love stories is the anthology *My Mistress's Sparrow is Dead* (edited by Jeffrey Eugenides, 2008).

- *Antony and Cleopatra* is a Shakespearean tragedy. Is it possible to compare the way Cleopatra mourns for Antony with any other Shakespearean character grieving for a departed beloved? Othello mourning Desdemona, for instance, or Lear grieving for Cordelia, his daughter?

- Consider which tense each writer chooses. 'Remember' is in the projected future tense, Kureishi's passage in the continuous present, and Cleopatra's lament is in the past. How does this affect our understanding?

- Consider the structure of each passage. Is there a change of mood during each passage?
  - a) The sonnet form provides us with the *volta*, the turn. Note that this occurs with the word 'Yet'. Is Rossetti giving the reader permission to mourn? Should one remember or forget?
  - b) The Kureishi extract has several turns, or changes of tone. For example, there are Rick's dark thoughts on the 'unloved', but the most unexpected turn is the arrival of the destined recipient of the message, the child himself, climbing into the frame. What is the impact of this?
  - c) Cleopatra appears to embellish a mythologically divine image of Antony, but she states firmly at the end that this transcends imagination and that this is Nature's work, grounded in truth and thus it is her Antony. Remember how many references there are to the natural world in her lexis – the ocean, thunder, winter, autumn. What is the effect?

Assignments

1 Consider the presentation of love at first sight in a range of texts you have studied. What similarities and differences do you detect in texts of different periods and genres?

2 James Fenton writes that 'a lyric poem expresses an intense feeling of the moment, and the truth of the poem consists of its truth to that moment'. How is intensity of feeling communicated in any love lyrics you have read? How convincing is the emotion conveyed?

3 Compile your own anthology of love poetry. Preface it by setting out the criteria for your selection and justify the inclusion of each poem selected.

4 Is there a significant difference between 'the literature of love' and 'love in literature'? Why do people talk comfortably about 'love poetry' but not about 'love novels'? Is the term ' romantic fiction' an adequate equivalent?

5 'Love stories depend on disappointment, on unequal births and feuding families, on matrimonial boredom and at least one cold heart,' writes Jeffrey Eugenides in the introduction to his collection of love stories *My Mistress's Sparrow is Dead*. Consider at least two love stories in the light of this statement.

6 Select three of the extracts in Part 3 and consider the ways in which writers communicate the torments of love. For example you might like to compare the extract from *Troilus and Criseyde* with the poem by Lady Mary Wroth and the extract from *Wuthering Heights*.

7 From your reading in the literature of love, what different methods do writers employ to express falling out of love? Compare 'The Crack' by Vicki Feaver with the extracts from *Portrait of a Lady* and *Their Eyes Were Watching God*.

8 'A never ending story.' How do writers conclude love stories? From your reading in the literature of love, compare several endings. What similarities do you notice? How often does love end in death?

6 | Resources

Further reading

Anthologies

A.D.P. Briggs, ed. *Love Please! One Hundred Passionate Poems* (Orion, 2001)
Anthology arranged in alphabetical order of poets.

James Fenton, ed. *The New Faber Book of Love Poems* (Faber and Faber, 2006)
Strong emphasis on lyric poetry and its 'affinity with music'.

Daisy Goodwin, ed. *The Nation's Favourite Love Poems* (BBC Books, 1998)
This survey of the nation's favourite love poems begins with the top ten. 'How do
I love thee' by Elizabeth Barrett Browning is Number One. Goodwin introduces the
book as 'an attempt to collect together everyone's favourite love poems', adding
'and wherever you've got to in the tunnel of love, remember that some poet has
been there before you'.

Josephine Hart, ed. *Catching Life by the Throat* (Virago, 2006)
Accessible selection of eight of the greatest poets in the English language, with
introductory essays and accompanying CD.

Francis Palgrave *The Golden Treasury* (Oxford Paperbacks, new edition 2002)
Contains, according to its editor, 'the best original lyric pieces and songs', arranged
chronologically from the Elizabethan lyricists to Wordsworth. The most popular
anthology from the Victorian period, regularly updated and still in print.

Virago Book of Love Poetry (Virago, 1998)
Anthology of poetry by women. Explores relationship between the lover and the
beloved 'Poetry knows no bounds between sacred and profane love.'

A.P. Wavell *Other Men's Flowers* (Jonathan Cape, 1944)
The title is borrowed from a sentence from the French essayist, Montaigne: 'I have
gathered a posie of other men's flowers and nothing but the thread that binds
them is my own.' Published during the Second World War and, like *The Golden
Treasury*, an enduringly popular anthology.

Short stories

Jeffrey Eugenides, ed. *My Mistress's Sparrow is Dead* (Harper Press, 2008)
Great love stories, from Chekhov to Alice Munro.

Penguin Great Loves (Penguin Classics, 2007)
Republication of romantic and erotic literature, including Virgil, Lawrence, Hardy and Updike.

John Sutherland, ed. *The Oxford Book of Love Stories* (Oxford University Press, 1996)

Reference and cultural context

J.A.Cuddon *The Penguin Dictionary of Literary Terms and Literary Theory* (Penguin, new edition 2004)

Andrew Dickson, ed. *The Rough Guide to Shakespeare* (Penguin, 2005)
Comprehensive user-friendly guide to plays, stage history, plots, background, critical approaches.

James Fenton, ed. *An Introduction to English Poetry* (Viking, 2002)
Indispensable guide to poetic form.

Stephen Fry *The Ode Less Travelled: Unlocking the Poet Within* (Hutchinson, 2005)
Further indispensable guide to poetic form.

Marcus Lodwick *The Gallery Companion: Understanding Western Art* (Thames and Hudson, 2002)
Provides stories behind western art, both classical and biblical. Explains symbolism.

Critical approaches

Peter Barry *Beginning Theory* (Manchester University Press, 1995)
Comprehensive guide to range of different critical approaches and theories. Invites readers to develop own ideas.

Catherine Belsey *Desire: Love Stories in Western Culture* (Blackwell, 1994)

Robert Eaglestone *Doing English* (Routledge, 2000)
Explains what we mean when we talk of 'doing English'. Looks at differences between traditional and recent theoretical approaches.

David Lodge *The Art of Fiction* (Penguin, 1992)
Demonstrates a range of technical terms.

Glossary

Blazon a list categorising and praising the different parts of (usually) a woman's body.

Carpe diem Latin (originally a phrase from Horace's Odes) meaning 'seize the day': it implies, 'Make the most of your youth. Life is short, death inevitable.'

Cuckold a deceived husband sprouting horns on his head. A figure of fun.

Elegy in classical literature a poem on a serious subject such as love, war or death, in rhyming metrical lines of different lengths. **Elegiac** suggests a mood of sadness and regret at saying farewell.

Epic a lengthy narrative poem on a heroic subject.

Epiphany moment of insight and revelation.

Fabliaux short, satirical comic narratives originating in France as a reaction against the courtly love tradition.

Fin amor in the vocabulary of courtly love, refined love.

Intertextual the implicit or explicit cross referencing of other texts in ways which enlarge one's awareness of the primary text.

Oxymoron from the Greek meaning sharp / foolish. A figure of speech combining two contradictory meanings.

Pre-lapsarian/ Post-lapsarian before and after the Fall, the moment Adam and Eve disobeyed God and ate the forbidden fruit from the Tree of Knowledge.

Prolepsis foreshadowing of events to come.

Villanelle same word derivation as *villain*, peasant. Originating in pastoral poetry, a villanelle has five three-line stanzas and a quatrain. The same rhyme echoes through the poem.

World of Forms (from Plato) the perfect world to which language aspires.

Zeugma from the Greek meaning 'joining'. A figure of speech in which a verb is applied, simultaneously and in different senses, to two other words.

Zeitgeist spirit of the age.

Index

Acknowledgements

The authors and publishers acknowledge the following sources of copyright material and are grateful for the permissions granted. While every effort has been made, it has not always been possible to identify the sources of all the material used, or to trace all copyright holders. If any omissions are brought to our notice, we will be happy to include the appropriate acknowledgements on reprinting.

pp. 83, 73, 74: Faber and Faber Ltd with Random House, Inc for W.H. Auden 'Alone' from *Collected Poems* by W.H. Auden. Copyright © 1941 and renewed 1969 by W.H. Auden; and with Farrar, Straus and Giroux, LLC for extracts from Ted Hughes '18 Rugby Street' and 'Robbing Myself' from *Birthday Letters* by Ted Hughes. Copyright © 1998 by Ted Hughes; and Ted Hughes 'To Sylvia Plath, 6 and 8 October, 1956' from *Letters of Ted Hughes* by Ted Hughes, selected and edited by Chistopher Reid. Copyright © 2007 by The Estate of Ted Hughes; pp. 68, 94–95: Little Brown and HarperCollins Publishers for extracts from Zora Neale Hurston *Their Eyes Were Watching God*, Virago (1986) pp. 259, 95–6. Copyright © 1937 by Harper & Row, Publishers, Inc, renewed © 1965 by John C. Hurston and Joel Hurston; p. 86: W.W. Norton & Company Ltd for E.E. Cummings, 'somewhere i have never travelled, gladly beyond' from *Complete Poems 1904–1962* by E.E. Cummings, ed. George J. Firmage. Copyright © 1991 by the Trustees for the E.E. Cummings Trust and George James Firmage; pp. 97–98: Penguin Books and The Wylie Agency on behalf of the Estate of the author for an extract from Evelyn Waugh *Brideshead Revisited: The Sacred and Profane Memories of Captain Charles Ryder*, first published by Chapman & Hall (1945), Penguin Classics (1999) pp. 234–5. Copyright © 1945 by Evelyn Waugh; p. 93: Random House Group Ltd for Vicky Feaver 'The Crack' from *The Handless Maiden* by Vicky Feaver, Jonathan Cape (1994); pp. 117–118: Rogers, Coleridge & White Ltd on behalf of the author for an extract from Hanif Kureishi 'Remember This Moment, Remember Us' from *The Body* by Hanif Kureishi, Faber & Faber (2002) pp. 229–231. Copyright © Hanif Kureishi; p. 34: United Agents on behalf of the author for extracts from James Fenton 'In Paris With You' from *Selected Poems* by James Fenton, Penguin Books (2006). Copyright © James Fenton 1994; pp. 50, 51: A.P. Watt Ltd on behalf of Grainne Yeats for extracts from W.B. Yeats 'The White Birds', 'The Song of the Wandering Aengus' and 'He Wishes for the Cloths of Heaven'